Dear God, Help Me Understand

Dear God, Help Me Understand

Real Questions from Real People

Though this book is designed for group study, it can be used for personal enjoyment and spiritual growth. A leader's guide is available from your local bookstore or from your publisher.

Beacon Hill Press of Kansas City
Kansas City, Mo.

Editor
Everett Leadingham

Editorial Assistant
Carolyn Clements

Editorial Committee
Randy Cloud
David Felter
Everett Leadingham
Thomas Mayse
Stephen M. Miller
Bryan Merrill
Carl Pierce
Gene Van Note

Copyright 1995
by Beacon Hill Press of Kansas City

ISBN 083-411-5417

Printed in the United States of America

Cover design by Triad Studio
Cover photo by Michael Griffitt

Bible Credits

Unless otherwise indicated, all Scripture quotations are taken from the *Holy Bible, New International Version*® (NIV®). Copyright © 1973, 1978, 1984 by International Bible Society. Used by permission of Zondervan Publishing House. All rights reserved.

The *New American Standard Bible* (NASB), © 1960, 1962, 1963, 1968, 1971, 1972, 1973, 1975, 1977 by The Lockman Foundation. Used by permission.

The Holy Bible, New Century Version (NCV), copyright © 1987, 1988, 1991 by Word Publishing, Dallas, Texas 75039. Used by permission.

New Revised Standard Version (NRSV) of the Bible, copyright 1989 by the Division of Christian Education of the National Council of the Churches of Christ in the USA. Used by permission. All rights reserved.

The New Testament in Modern English (Phillips), Revised Student Edition, by J. B. Phillips, translator. Copyright 1958, 1960, 1972 by J. B. Phillips. Reprinted with the permission of the Macmillan Publishing Company.

The *Revised Standard Version* (RSV) of the Bible, copyright 1946, 1952, 1971 by the Division of Christian Education of the National Council of the Churches of Christ in the USA. Used by permission.

The King James Version (KJV).

10   9   8   7   6   5   4   3   2

Contents

Introduction..7

1   Ask Him Anything 9
    Lloyd John Ogilvie

2   Is God Unfair? 21
    Philip Yancey

3   What's Going On in Heaven Right Now?.............33
    Gene Van Note

4   What Makes Us What We Are?....................45
    Les Parrott III

5   Where Is God in Addiction? 55
    Paul Fitzgerald

6   This Schedule's Killing Us! 67
    Bonnie Perry

7   Should I Speak Up?...................................77
    Ed Robinson

8   The Good News of the Unpardonable Sin 85
    Carl Leth

9   Does Prayer Really Change Anything? 93
    George Lyons

10 Will Somebody Please Stop the Violence? 103
    Rebecca Laird

11 God Has a Wonderful Plan for Your Life 115
    Randall Davey

12 Never Too Old 125
    Vicki Hesterman

13 Will I Only Be Remembered if My Name's
    in the News?..137
    Doug Williams

Introduction

Each chapter of this book begins with a question, a tough question that we wish God would answer directly. But He hasn't. He has revealed answers that hint at our specific questions. He has left it to us to discover the personal meaning for our situations today.

The questions come from folks like you and me, persons with real lives, real cares, real joys. A questionnaire was sent to a variety of holiness churches, and 13 of the most thought-provoking questions were chosen for this book. Some questions were signed, some not—but all are real. Though many of the questions are very specific, and sometimes very personal, they open the door for us to talk about broader issues.

We turned some of our best "thinkers" loose on these questions. Drawing from the Bible, research, and their personal expertise, these writers have shed light on the wider concerns suggested by the questions asked. But they have not—they could not—answer everything. Now it's your turn. So, strap on your "thinking cap" and get ready for lively discussion of some of life's important questions. Because in this confusing life, every sincere Christian wants to pray: "Dear God, help me understand."

THE  UESTION

"Is it OK for Christians to question God?"

THE | SSUES

- What is God really like?
- How can we have free will if God knows everything in advance?
- Can we ever really know anything about God?

BACKGROUND SCRIPTURE:

Isa. 40

1

Ask Him Anything

by Lloyd John Ogilvie

IT WAS A STARTLING conversation with an old friend. He looked me in the eye and said, "Lloyd, I've been a closet agnostic for some time now. I used to be so sure of what I believed, but now I have to admit I've known *about* God, but never really known God. I've got so many unanswered questions. I guess my mind has finally caught up with my heart!"

I should not have been surprised. Now, as I look back over the years, I can see that there were clear danger signals. The man's simplistic and traditional religion had never grappled with life's deepest questions—the tough intellectual questions that defy easy answers. He had evaded them, thinking that to question was to deny faith. Then personal difficulties, problems with other people, and anguish over the immense tragedies of the world had hit him with hurricane force and sent him into a tailspin of doubt and discouragement. He had lived in two worlds: one of vague, cultural religion, and the other of profound, unresolved questions. When his worlds collided, he realized God was not very real to him.

Adapted from the chapters "What Is God Like?" and "Is God Really in Control?" in *Ask Him Anything*, Lloyd J. Ogilvie, 1981, Word Inc., Dallas, Tex. All rights reserved. Used by permission.

Questions About God

Agnosticism is the silent agony of our age. It's not questions about God's existence that trouble most people, but questions about what He is like and how they can know Him. The unanswered questions about God, about His nature, will, and ways have surfaced as an honest but very unsatisfying, "I just don't know!" And this uncertainty troubles people both inside and outside the church.

It's when our lives sour or the suffering of the world stabs us awake that we realize we do not really know the God in whom others profess to believe. The animated question marks of our existence stir the brewing agnosticism in our minds. We are like Kipling's "Elephant Child":

> She sends 'em abroad on her own affairs
> From the second she opens her eyes.
> One million hows, two million wheres
> And seven million whys.

All our hows and wheres and whys eventually lead back to questions about God—about some aspect of His nature and relationship to His creation. That's the conviction that gripped me as I was studying to respond to the thousands of questions submitted by my congregation and television viewers. Then, after weeks of reading, praying, and aching over each question, it came to me. As I watched the sun rise one morning, I realized with sudden clarity that *every* question I had been struggling with was rooted in a need to know God, how He acts, and what He has said about himself. Whether the question was about the *where* of God in our needs, the *why* of suffering, or the *how* of the origin or extent of evil, the answer was hidden in God himself.

The questions about unanswered prayer, why bad things happen to good people, the dark night of the soul's doubt, how to find guidance and to live abundantly were all, in one sense, *agnostic* questions about God. Every question, from how to pray to how to stop worrying and start living, was a rearticulation of the deeper question: "What is God like—and how can I know Him?" That's why we must begin our search for answers to life's most urgent questions by getting to know God.

The Source of Our Questions

Actually, I am convinced God is the author of, as well as the answer to, our aching questions. It is because He is at work in us that we even dare to question! Honest, intellectual questioning is a sign of growth, not denial. God wants us to get in touch with the questions that have kept us from growing spiritually. Our questions reflect our inbred, divine desire to grow. God knows that if we dare to think, eventually our questions will lead us to Him and into the profound relationship with Him for which we were created.

Essentially, I believe life's biggest questions are the result of the fact that our [concept of] God has been too small, our vision of Him too limited. Therefore, the only antidote to our quandary of questions is to learn to fully acknowledge God's greatness. That was Paternus' advice to his son: "First of all, my child, think magnificently of God. Magnify His providence; adore His power; pray to Him frequently and incessantly. Bear Him always in your mind; teach your thoughts to reverence Him in every place, for there is no place where He is not. Therefore, my child, fear and worship, and love God; first and last, think magnificently of God."

Failing to "think magnificently" was Israel's problem during the excruciating experience of the Babylonian exile following the destruction of Jerusalem in 586 B.C. The Holy City had been razed, and the Hebrew people were led out of their cherished Palestine into the idol-worshiping land of pagan Babylonia. They were forced to realize how agnostic they had been about their God. Anguishing questions surged to the surface. How could God allow this to happen? Were they not His chosen, cherished people? Why did the innocent have to suffer along with the guilty? Did God know or care about their plight and the unquenchable longing for their homeland? Did His sovereignty extend beyond Palestine to heathen places such as Babylonia? Their world had been blown to pieces, and their questions were pulling them apart.

Israel's limited concept of God as only the Lord of Palestine was the root cause of their anxiety and fear—all their wrenching questions. And God's own answer in Isa. 40, particularly verses 25-31, was His answer to pull them together. It gives us the basis of thinking magnificently about God. The exciting thing about this passage is that it proclaims God's greatness and His grace, His might, and His mercy; His almightiness and His availability, His power and His presence. It begins with His sovereignty and ends with the strength we experience when we truly know Him.

God Is Holy

Thinking magnificently about God begins with His holiness. In response to our questions about what He is like, He counters with a mind-expanding question: "'To whom then will you liken Me that I should be his equal?' says the Holy One" (Isa. 40:25). Both the question and the name of the questioner confront us with the holiness of God. His holiness is separate, distinct, and beyond the categories of human definition. Whatever words we use to define His nature fall short of His greatness. He is not the object of our search but the Subject of His own revelation. All we can know of the Holy Other is what He tells us about himself.

With God there is always mystery. And remember that an aspect of the word mystery in Greek means, "To shut one's mouth." Awe and wonder, coupled with praise and adoration, is the appropriate response to the holiness of God. He is the unmoved Mover, the uncreated Creator of the universe. In Him all things congeal and are held together. As a great scientist put it, "If God stopped breathing, the universe would disintegrate."

The awareness of God's greatness and holiness is what the Hebrew people languishing in Babylonia needed to recapture. God was not one among many gods. He is the Holy One—greater than any image formed by human hand or any words articulated by human tongue. And that's where we must begin. God is greater than we are—greater than the false gods of our culture, greater than the theological formulations we have written about Him or the religious customs we have developed to worship Him.

God Is Great

That leads to a renewed sense of wonder and the second attribute of God that enables us to think magnificently of Him. Listen to the prophet's challenge to the homesick Hebrews. In Babylonia, their God was now in competition with Marduk, the Babylonian god of creation and the lesser gods of Babylonian religion. Each of these many deities was believed to dwell among the stars, and the stars were named after them.

Into this polytheistic confusion, the prophet gives the trumpet blast of praise to the Holy One who alone is Creator of the universe, the One who fixed the stars in their places. "Lift up your eyes on high and see who has created these stars, the One who leads forth their host by number, He calls them by name; because of the greatness of His might and the strength of His power. Not one of them is missing" (Isa. 40:26). It was as if He was saying, "Look up! Lift your drooping hearts and think magnificently of God as the Creator of the universe. If He knows all the stars by name and is greater than all the Babylonian gods, He knows each of you. God will take care of you!"

The greatness of God is revealed in His creation. The vastness of His universe engenders a sense of wonder. Think of it! If we were to drive a car day and night at top speed without stopping, it would take us 9 years to reach the moon, 300 years to reach the sun, 8,300 years to reach the planet Neptune, 27 million years to reach Alpha Centauri, and 700 million years to reach the Pole Star.

This is the reason the psalmist could say, "When I consider Thy heavens, the work of Thy fingers, the moon and the stars, which Thou hast ordained; what is man, that Thou dost take thought of him? And the son of man, that Thou dost care for him? Yet Thou hast made him a little lower than God, and dost crown him with glory and majesty!" (Ps. 8:3-5). Who wouldn't be astonished by that?

I've found that standing and staring at creation and then contemplating my own unique and special individuality by God's design, helps me think magnificently of God and helps put my world in perspective. Yeats said in his autobiography, "Can one reach God by toil? He gives himself to the pure in heart. He asks nothing but our attention." Has your Creator caught your attention?

God Knows Everything

But press on! Next think magnificently of the omniscience of God. He is all-knowing. It is awesome to think of His holiness and astounding to contemplate His creation, but it is both alarming and assuring to reflect on His omniscience. To a bereft and depleted people who thought they were forgotten by their God, Isaiah questions: "Why do you say, O Jacob, and assert, O Israel, 'My way is hidden from the LORD, and the justice due me escapes the notice of my God'? Do you not know? Have you not heard? The Everlasting God, the LORD, the Creator of the ends of the earth does not become weary or tired. His understanding is inscrutable" (40:27-28).

God knows all about us. He knows our deepest inner hopes and dreams, our fears and frustrations, our desires and disappointments. He knows us absolutely and utterly. He sees into us with x-ray vision.

The prophet draws on the magnificence of God's omniscience as a great source of comfort for His people. They could trust their God for vindication and ultimately for victory. God was in control. He would have the final word. That's what we all need to know when life falls apart or when we feel the injustice of life.

God Is Powerful

And yet, knowledge of God's omniscience is of little comfort without an assurance of His omnipotence. It's one thing to know that God is aware of our needs, but another to be confident He has the power to act in our behalf. But note the names Isaiah uses in this passage for the God of Israel. He is "the LORD"—*Yahweh* in Hebrew, from the essential verb meaning "to be." He is the God who makes things happen, who wields sovereign authority. His power is revealed in creation and history. He is everlasting, without beginning and end, the One in whom all power resides, and He is greater than the gods of the Babylonians as well as their kings and rulers.

In verse 28, the names "Everlasting God" and "Creator" are kept together around the fulcrum name *Yahweh* ("the LORD"), because they express the fact that He is God over time and space, and yet has been constantly involved in caring for His people. He is worthy of His people waiting for Him to act with power for their deliverance. God, who is everlasting, has been infinitely patient with His people; now they are called to wait patiently for Him to act. The omnipotent, powerful Yahweh never grows weary.

That assurance leads to one of the most encouraging of the attributes of God. Think magnificently of the fact that God who has all power entrusts strength to us when we are weary. The people who were completely exhausted and without strength were given a great promise: "He gives strength to the weary, and to him who lacks might, He increases power" (v. 29). This passage focuses on the weakness of Israel and on the strength of their God. It emphasizes that human strength is always inadequate and limited, that even young men grow weary and tired and stumble. But then it continues with its magnificent words of assurance: "Those who wait for the LORD will gain new strength; they will mount up with wings like eagles, they will run and not get tired, they will walk and not become weary" (v. 31). God knows, He acts with power, and He entrusts that power to His people.

I want to emphasize one point about an eagle's flight that is crucial to this passage. The eagle soars when it is caught up in the stream of the wind. It does not soar in its own strength. The bird's innate capacity to fly is multiplied by the power of the wind, which lifts and impels it. So it is with us when we wait for God. God's Spirit has the power to infuse the tissues of our impotent minds, our depleted emotions, our wayward wills, our weary bodies. God's omnipotent power is gloriously revealed in the energizing, vitalizing, and uplifting of our human nature; we were created to be inadequate until filled with His magnificence.

From the Isa. 40 passage, what answers to the question, "What is God like?" can we glean? We get a vivid picture of the magnificence of God. He is holy, hidden—but revealed to us because He has chosen to make himself known. He is the Creator, the Lord of the universe. He is all-knowing and all-powerful, and He gives supporting strength to us when our own strength fails.

All these words—holy, creative, omniscient, omnipotent—can be used to explain what God is like. We should always keep them in mind as we honestly explore our faith in God.

How Is God Involved with Us?

Furthermore, three presuppositions must guide our answer to all the questions about God's involvement in our troubled world and our often-calamitous existence. First, God is *supremely* in control when He limits His control. Second, He is *sensitively* in control as He grants us the gift of free will, knowing what we may do with it. Third, He is *sublimely* in control as He intervenes and brings good out of evil that happens to and around us.

Fortified with these three gigantic truths about the nature of God, we can confront the disquiet within us about the checkered record of history and about our own topsy-turvy lives with their concerns, crises, and complications.

"If God is almighty, why doesn't He do better?" some have asked. That brash question might be stated more delicately by others of us: "Lord, why don't You make life a little bit better?" But the question is the same. We struggle to balance three other true, but time-tarnished assumptions: that God is *omnipotent*, having all power; *omniscient*, having all knowledge; and *gracious*, having all love. We are often tempted to sacrifice one or more of these three rocks of our intellectual and spiritual foundation in seeking to explain what we go through and what happens in the world around us. If God is all-loving, all-powerful, and all-knowing, why doesn't He do what we want when we think we need it? Unable to endure what was meant to be creative insecurity leading to faithful trust, we say with sophomoric persistence, "Either God is all-powerful and not all-knowing, or He is all-knowing and not all-powerful."

But what happened to the "all-loving" leg of the tripod? That's the secret: absolute love guides the Lord's exercise of His omniscience and omnipotence in the affairs of His people. What He does with what He knows is always conditioned by what decisions will enable us to become mature, healthy persons. Greatness of character and personality is not produced by a smooth, easy life. It is in the difficulties as much as in the delights of life that we are forced to grow. The sure conviction of my life after over 30 years of experiencing God's providence is this: He never allows more than we can stand. He uses all that happens to us to bring us into deeper trust and dependence on Him, and His interventions are perfectly timed to help us without negating our freedom.

We've been reluctant to grapple with the implications of the paradox of God's control and our freedom. We've clutched one side or another of the paradox. There's been a softness in our thinking. We put God on trial for the things He's allowed, wondering why He's not done better, only to find that we are the ones on trial . . . and He's the judge. We throw the ball to Him, demanding explanations about how He's running the universe, only to find He throws it back to us. God is the pitcher, not the catcher, of our hard questions about the condition of humanity. But we find it difficult to catch; our fists are clenched with arrogant consternation over the state of the world. And if we do dare to catch, what God pitches stings our gloves!

The truth we must catch, however much it hurts, is that God had to give us freedom, knowing what we might do with it. There is no alternative; we had to be either puppets or persons. Because of His love for us, God wants us to be persons. And so we must dare to be what He created us to be, with all the dangers of misusing our freedom.

The great assurance is that He does not leave us alone with that freedom. He loves us so much that He uses the circumstances He allows to happen to help us grow. He will not deny us the depth of maturity that comes in the things that force us to cry out, "God, help me!" Be sure of this: nothing will ever happen that will not ultimately be used to help us claim our destiny as cocreators with God in shaping a person to live with Him abundantly, now and eternally. Then, in partnership with Him, we can work with relentless zeal to communicate His love to others. We can become indefatigable in the use of our freedom to live under His rule, proclaiming the kingdom of God in all our realms of responsibility.

Christ Reveals God to Us

This is all summed up in a significant way when we focus our thinking on the magnificence of God in Christ; we meet Him face-to-face! He is not distant or aloof. In fact, He is the initiator of all our thoughts about Him. He has had each of us on His mind since the foundation of the world. All the questions we can ask will find more than a conceptual answer. We will find Him because He has already found us. But truth *about* God will never satisfy us. It only becomes real as we live it by giving all of ourselves to know Him personally. How would you live the rest of your life if you really believed all that we've said about God thus far? When we think magnificently about God, we will build our lives on His greatness:

As the marsh hen secretly builds on the water sod,
Behold I will build me a nest on the greatness of God . . .
By so many roots as the marsh-grass sends in the sod,
I will heartily lay me a hold on the greatness of God.
(Sidney Lanier, "The Marshes of Glynn")

All Scripture quotations in this article are taken from the *New American Standard Bible* (NASB).

THE **Q**UESTION

*"Why does God allow bad things
to happen to good people?"*

THE **I**SSUES

- Why doesn't an all-powerful God do
  something about suffering?
- Why do such stressful situations happen to
  some persons but not to others?
- How can we cope in such situations?

BACKGROUND SCRIPTURE:

Job 2; 21

2

Is God Unfair?

by Philip Yancey

*T*HE ROAD LESS TRAVELED, by M. Scott Peck, opens with a blunt, three-word sentence: "Life is difficult." If reduced to a single sentence, the Book of Job would express something similar, for the loud cry, "Life is unfair!" resounds from almost every page.

Unfairness is no easier for us to swallow today than it was for Job thousands of years ago. We make an instinctive judgment that life *ought* to be fair and that God should somehow "do a better job" of running His world.

The world as it is versus the world as it ought to be— the constant tension between those two states—bursts into the open in the Book of Job. For three long, windy rounds, Job and his friends spar in a verbal boxing match. On the ground rules, they all agree: God should reward those who do good and punish those who do evil.

Why, then, is Job, a supposedly good man, suffering so much apparent punishment? Job's friends, confident of God's fairness, defend the world as it is. "Use your common sense," they tell Job. "God would not afflict you without a cause. You must have committed some secret sin." But Job, who knows beyond doubt he has done nothing to deserve such punishment, cannot agree. He pleads innocent.

Gradually, however, the suffering wears down Job's most cherished beliefs. How can God be on his side? Job wonders. He is, after all, squatting in a heap of ashes, the ruins of his life. He is a broken, despairing man, "betrayed" by God. "Look at me and be astonished; clap your hand over your mouth," Job cries (21:5).

A crisis of faith brews inside him. Is God unfair? Such a notion calls into question everything Job believes, but how else can he explain what has happened? He looks around for other examples of unfairness and sees that evil people sometimes do prosper—they don't get punished, as he'd like to believe—while some godly people suffer. And many other people live happy, fruitful lives without ever giving a thought to God. For Job, the facts simply do not add up. "When I think about this, I am terrified; trembling seizes my body" (21:6).

The reason the Book of Job seems so modern is that for us, too, the facts do not add up. Job's strident message of life's unfairness seems peculiarly suited to our own pain-racked century. Simply plug contemporary illustrations into his arguments: "innocent" but starving children in the Third World; faithful pastors imprisoned in South Africa; Christian leaders who die in their prime; spoiled entertainers who profit obscenely from flouting God's rules; the millions in Western Europe who live quiet, happy lives and never give God a thought. Far from fading away, Job's questions about this world's unfairness have only grown louder and shriller. We still expect a God of love and power to follow certain rules on earth. Why doesn't He?

Coming to Terms with Unfairness

At some point, every human being confronts the mysteries that caused Job to tremble in terror. Is God unfair?

One option seemed obvious to Job's wife: "Curse God and die!" she advised (2:9). Why hold on to a sentimental belief in a loving God when so much in life conspires against it? And in this Job-like century, more people than ever before have come to agree with her. Some Jewish writers, such as Jerzy Kosinski and Elie Wiesel, began with a strong faith in God but saw it vaporize in the gas furnaces of the Holocaust. Face-to-face with history's grossest unfairness, they concluded that God must not exist. (Still, the human instinct asserts itself. Kosinski and Wiesel cannot avoid a tone of outrage, as if they, too, feel betrayed. They overlook the underlying issue of where our primal sense of fairness comes from. Why ought we even to *expect* the world to be fair?)

Others, equally mindful of the world's unfairness, cannot bring themselves to deny God's existence. Instead, they propose another possibility: perhaps God agrees that life is unfair, but cannot do anything about it. Rabbi Harold Kushner took this approach in his best-selling book *When Bad Things Happen to Good People*. After watching his son die of the disease progeria, Kushner concluded that "even God has a hard time keeping chaos in check," and that God is "a God of justice and not of power."

According to Rabbi Kushner, God is as frustrated, even outraged, by the unfairness on this planet as anyone else, but He lacks the power to change it. Millions of readers found comfort in Kushner's portrayal of a God who seemed compassionate, albeit weak. I wonder, however, what those people make of the last five chapters of Job, which contain God's "self-defense." No other part of the Bible conveys God's power so impressively. If God is less than powerful, why did He choose the worst possible situation, when His power was most called into question, to insist on His omnipotence? (Elie Wiesel said of the God described by Kushner, "If that's who God is, why doesn't He resign and let someone more competent take His place?")

A third group of people evades the problem of unfairness by looking to the future, when an exacting justice will work itself out in the universe. Unfairness is a temporary condition, they say. The Hindu doctrine of Karma, which applies a mathematical precision to this belief, calculates it may take a soul 6,800,000 incarnations to realize perfect justice. At the end of all those incarnations, a person will have experienced exactly the amount of pain and pleasure that he or she deserves.

A fourth approach is to flatly deny the problem and insist the world is fair. Echoing Job's friends, these people insist the world does run according to fixed, regular laws: good people will prosper and evil ones will fail. I encountered this point of view at a faith-healing church in Indiana, and I hear it virtually every time I watch religious television, where some evangelist promises perfect health and financial prosperity to anyone who asks for it in true faith.

Such lavish promises have obvious appeal, but they fail to account for all the facts. The babies who contract AIDS *in utero,* for example, or the roll call of persecuted saints in *Foxe's Book of Martyrs*—how do these fit into a doctrine of life's fairness? There is nothing I would rather have said to Meg Woodson [whose daughter died of cystic fibrosis] than, "The world is fair, and therefore if you pray hard enough, your daughter will not die." But I could not say that, any more than I can now say, "God took Peggie away because of something you did wrong." Both points of view are represented in the Book of Job; both are dismissed by God in the end.

It takes an Olympian leap of faith to argue that life is completely fair. More commonly, Christians respond to life's unfairness not by denying it outright but by watering it down. They, like Job's friends, search for some hidden reason behind suffering:

"God is trying to teach you something. You should feel privileged, not bitter, about your opportunity to lean on Him in faith."

"Meditate on the blessings you still enjoy—at least you are alive. Are you a fair-weather believer?"

"You are undergoing a training regimen, a chance to exercise new muscles of faith. Don't worry—God will not test you beyond your endurance."

"Don't complain so loudly! You will forfeit this opportunity to demonstrate your faithfulness to nonbelievers."

"Someone is always worse off than you. Give thanks despite your circumstances."

Job's friends offered a version of each of these words of wisdom, and each contains an element of truth. But the Book of Job plainly shows that such "helpful advice" does nothing to answer the question of the person in pain. It was the wrong medicine, dispensed at the wrong time.

And finally, there is one more way to explain the world's unfairness. After hearing all the alternatives, Job was driven to the conclusion I have suggested as the one-sentence summary of the entire book: *Life is unfair!* It came to Job more as a reflex reaction than a philosophy of life, and that is how it strikes anyone who suffers. "Why me?" we ask. "What have I done?"

A Modern Job

While working on this question, I made it a point to meet regularly with people who felt betrayed by God. I wanted to keep before me the actual look, the facial expressions, of disappointment and doubt. When it came time to write about the Book of Job, I decided to interview the one person I know whose life most resembles Job's, a man I will call Douglas.

To me, Douglas seems "righteous" in the same sense as Job: not perfect, of course, but a model of faithfulness. After years of training in psychotherapy, he had declined a lucrative career in favor of starting an urban ministry. Douglas's troubles began some years ago when his wife discovered a lump in her breast. Surgeons removed that breast, but two years later the cancer had spread to her lungs. Douglas took over many household and parental duties as his wife battled the debilitating effects of chemotherapy. Sometimes she couldn't hold down any food. She lost her hair. And always she felt tired and vulnerable to fear and depression.

One night, in the midst of this crisis, as Douglas was driving down a city street with his wife and 12-year-old daughter, a drunk driver swerved across the center line and smashed head-on into their car. Douglas's wife was badly shaken, but unhurt. His daughter suffered a broken arm and severe facial cuts from windshield glass. Douglas himself received the worst injury, a massive blow to the head.

After the accident, Douglas never knew when a headache might strike. He could not work a full day and sometimes he would become disoriented and forgetful. Worse, the accident permanently affected his vision. One eye wandered at will, refusing to focus. He developed double vision and could hardly walk down a flight of stairs without assistance. Douglas learned to cope with all his disabilities but one: he could not read more than a page or two at a time. All his life, he had loved books. Now he was restricted to the limited selections and the sluggish pace of recorded books.

When I called Douglas to ask for an interview, he suggested meeting over breakfast; and when the scheduled time came, I braced myself for a difficult morning. By then I had interviewed a dozen people and had heard the full range of disappointment with God. If anyone had a right to be angry at God, Douglas did. Just that week, his wife had gotten a dismaying report from the hospital: there was another spot on her lung.

As our meal was being served, we caught up on the details of our lives. Douglas ate with great concentration and care. Thick glasses corrected some of his vision problems, but he had to work hard at focusing just to guide his fork to his mouth. I forced myself to look directly at him as he talked, trying to ignore the distraction of his wandering eye. At last, as we finished breakfast and motioned to the waitress for more coffee, I described my work on disappointment with God. "Could you tell me about your own disappointment?" I asked. "What have you learned that might help someone else going through a difficult time?"

Douglas was silent for what seemed like a long time. He stroked his peppery gray beard and gazed off beyond my right shoulder. I fleetingly wondered if he was having a mental "gap." Finally he said, "To tell you the truth, Philip, I didn't feel any disappointment with God."

I was startled. Douglas, searingly honest, had always rejected easy formulas like the "Turn your scars into stars!" testimonials of religious television. I waited for him to explain.

"The reason is this. I learned, first through my wife's illness and then especially through the accident, not to confuse God with life. I'm no stoic. I am as upset about what happened to me as anyone could be. I feel free to curse the unfairness of life and to vent all my grief and anger. But I believe God feels the same way about that accident— grieved and angry. I don't blame Him for what happened."

Douglas continued, "I have learned to see beyond the

physical reality in this world to the spiritual reality. We tend to think, 'Life should be fair because God is fair.' But God is not life. And if I confuse God with the physical reality of life—by expecting constant good health, for example—then I set myself up for a crashing disappointment.

"God's existence, even His love for me, does not depend on my good health. Frankly, I've had more time and opportunity to work on my relationship with God during my impairment than before."

There was a deep irony in that scene. For months I had been absorbed in the failures of faith, having sought out stories of people disappointed in God. I had chosen Douglas as my modern Job and had expected from him a bitter blast of protest. The last thing I anticipated was a graduate-school course in faith.

"If we develop a relationship with God *apart* from our life circumstances," said Douglas, "then we may be able to hang on when the physical reality breaks down. We can learn to trust God despite all the unfairness of life. Isn't that really the main point of Job?"

Although Douglas's strict separation of "physical reality" and "spiritual reality" bothered me, I found his notion intriguing. For the next hour, we worked through the Bible together, testing out his ideas. In the Sinai wilderness, God's guarantees of *physical* success—health, prosperity, and military victory—did nothing to help the Israelites' *spiritual* performance. And most heroes of the Old Testament (Abraham, Joseph, David, Elijah, Jeremiah, Daniel) went through trials much like Job's. For each of them, at times, the physical reality surely seemed to present God as the enemy. But each managed to hold on to a trust in Him despite the hardships. In doing so, their faith moved from a "contract faith"—I'll follow God if He treats me well—to a relationship that could transcend any hardship.

Suddenly, Douglas glanced at his watch and realized he was already late for another appointment. He put his coat on hurriedly and stood up to leave, and then leaned forward with one final thought. "I challenge you to go home and read again the story of Jesus. Was life 'fair' to Him? For me, the Cross demolished for all time the basic assumption that life will be fair."

Douglas and I had started out discussing Job and ended up discussing Jesus, and that pattern stayed with me: in the Old Testament one of God's favorites suffered terrible unfairness, and in the New Testament God's own Son suffered even more.

When I returned home, I took Douglas's advice and went through the Gospels again, wondering how Jesus would have answered the direct question, "Is life unfair?" Nowhere did I find Him denying unfairness. When Jesus encountered a sick person, He never delivered a lecture about "accepting your lot in life"; He healed whoever approached Him. And His scathing words about the rich and powerful of His day show clearly what He thought about social inequities. The Son of God reacted to life's unfairness much like anybody else. When He met a person in pain, He was deeply moved with compassion. When His friend Lazarus died, He wept. When Jesus himself faced suffering, He recoiled from it, asking three times if there was any other way.

God responded to the question of unfairness not with words but with a visit, an Incarnation. And Jesus offers flesh-and-blood proof of how God feels about unfairness, for He took on the "stuff" of life, the physical reality at its unfairest. He gave, in summary, a final answer to all lurking questions about the goodness of God. (It occurred to me as I read the Gospels that if all of us in His Body would spend our lives as He did—ministering to the sick, feeding the hungry, resisting the powers of evil, comforting those who mourn, and bringing the good news of love and forgiveness—then perhaps the question, "Is God unfair?" would not be asked with such urgency today.)

The Great Unfairness

Is God unfair? The answer depends on how closely we identify God and life. Surely life on earth is unfair. Douglas was correct in saying that the Cross settled that issue forever.

Author Henri Nouwen tells the story of a family he knew in Paraguay. The father, a doctor, spoke out against the military regime there and its human rights abuses. Local police took their revenge on him by arresting his teenage son and torturing him to death. Enraged townsfolk wanted to turn the boy's funeral into a huge protest march, but the doctor chose another means of protest. At the funeral, the father displayed his son's body as he had found it in the jail—naked, scarred from the electric shocks and cigarette burns and beatings. All the villagers filed past the corpse, which lay not in a coffin but on the blood-soaked mattress from the prison. It was the strongest protest imaginable, for it put injustice on grotesque display.

Isn't that what God did at Calvary? "It's God who ought to suffer, not you and me," say those who bear a grudge against God for the unfairness of life. The Cross that held Jesus' body, naked and marked with scars, exposed all the violence and injustice of this world. At once, the Cross revealed what kind of world we have and what kind of God we have: a world of gross unfairness, a God of sacrificial love.

No one is exempt from tragedy or disappointment— God himself was not exempt. Jesus offered no immunity, no way *out* of the unfairness, but rather a way *through* it to the other side. Just as Good Friday demolished the instinctive belief that this life is supposed to be fair, Easter Sunday followed with its startling clue to the riddle of the universe. Out of the darkness, a bright light shone.

The primal desire for fairness dies hard, and it should. Who among us does not sometimes yearn for more justice in this world here and now? Secretly, I admit, I yearn for a world "fault-proof" against disappointment, a world where my magazine articles will always find acceptance and my body does not grow old and weak, a world where my sister-in-law does not deliver a brain-damaged child, and where Peggie Woodson lives into ripe old age. But if I stake my faith on such a fault-proof earth, my faith will let me down. Even the greatest of miracles do not resolve the problems of this earth: all people who find physical healing eventually die.

We need more than miracles. We need a new heaven and a new earth, and until we have those, unfairness will not disappear.

A friend of mine, struggling to believe in a loving God amid much pain and sorrow, blurted out this statement: "God's only excuse is Easter!" The language is nontheological and harsh, but within that phrase lies a haunting truth. The cross of Christ may have overcome evil, but it did not overcome unfairness. For that, Easter is required. Someday, God will restore all physical reality to its proper place under His reign. Until then, it is a good thing to remember that we live out our days on Easter *Saturday*.

THE UESTION

*"What is George doing? Does he miss me?
Does he ask You about me and the children?"*

THE SSUES

- Where are the dead? Are they conscious?
- What is heaven like? What activity happens there?
- Will we know our families when we get to heaven?

BACKGROUND SCRIPTURE:

Luke 16:19-31; 24:31, 39; John 20:19; Acts 7:55-60;
1 Cor. 15:42-57

3

What's Going On in Heaven Right Now?

by Gene Van Note

JOE'S DEAD! Hit by a train!"

Those words screamed into the telephone shattered my Sunday afternoon. Joe, an impulsive 11-year-old boy, died the way he lived—on the edge of danger. Only this time he got too close. Joe rode around the warning gates and the caboose just as the train passed. He was looking over his shoulder at his little brother, Bobby, when he rode his bicycle in front of a second train. No one was at fault. No one was blamed. A boy took a careless chance—and lost his life.

I was a very young pastor, but that wasn't the first time I had faced death with my church family. It was, however, the first time I couldn't use comments like, "She is at peace, at last." Or, "He lived a long life; this is the way he would have wanted it."

Gene Van Note is the former executive editor of adult curriculum at the Church of the Nazarene International Headquarters. He retired in 1994 and lives in Overland Park, Kansas.

The night before Joe's funeral I sat with the family in the kitchen of their home. Anguish had drained the fountain of tears. Only silence remained. Joe's mother held a cold cup of coffee as tenderly as if it were her lost boy. Finally, without looking up, she said quietly, "Would you please talk to Bobby. He keeps asking, 'Where's Joe now? What's he doin'?' I don't know how to answer him."

I didn't have any answers either. No professor ever talked about those questions while I was in college or seminary. Or if he did, I don't remember what he said.

Bobby and I went outside and sat on the front steps. I still remember what I said to that eight-year-old. The words are too painful to forget. Nor can I dismiss the fact that I compounded Bobby's grief. I couldn't help the little guy. My words were as meaningless to him as they were to me.

But his questions still cry out for answers. What does the Christian faith have to say to all those in grief who ask them? That is our quest in this chapter.

Easy Questions to Ask; Tough to Answer

"Death is a black camel that kneels once at every man's door," says an ancient Turkish proverb. Sooner or later the door is opened for everyone. When that happens, we have no choice but to climb on the black camel for a one-way trip into the trackless desert.

Death reinforces our limitations. Luke records a story Jesus told about the afterlife. In the middle of it lies a statement that highlights our humanity. Jesus said, "A great chasm has been fixed, so that those who want to go from here [life] to you [death] cannot" (Luke 16:26).

The finality of death haunts us. C. S. Lewis expressed this pain eloquently in *A Grief Observed,* where he records the intensely personal account of his reaction to the death of his wife. "No one ever told me that grief felt so like fear.

I am not afraid, but the sensation is like being afraid. The same fluttering in the stomach, the same restlessness, the yawning. I keep on swallowing. There is an invisible blanket between the world and me."[1]

Later in the same account he writes, "The sharp, cleansing tang of her otherness is gone. What pitiable cant* to say, 'She will live forever in my memory!' *Live*—that is exactly what she won't do."[2]

A Magnificent Mystery

We should not suppose that we can do what no one has ever done before—answer all the questions our active minds or troubled spirits can ask. Many of the questions we ask each other in our sorrow, and sometimes in our anger, are unanswerable because the explanation has its feet in a dramatically different kind of reality. The apostle Paul wrote, "Now we see but a poor reflection as in a mirror; then we shall see face to face. Now I know in part; then I shall know fully, even as I am fully known" (1 Cor. 13:12).

And so we face a mystery. The fact that the mystery exists is encouraging. It shouts to all who listen that this universe is not limited to the dimensions of even our brightest and best-trained minds. The mystery gives us hope. And, for that reason, it is a magnificent mystery.

Our Search for Answers Is Very Human

Certainly it is normal for persons suffering in the inky blackness of grief to want someone to turn on the light. **We push against the edges of the mystery we call "death" and wonder what lies beyond.** In our search, we sense that life and death are not the same for everyone. Some people have found a way to live that transcends the anguish of their loss. A hospital worker, commenting on

---

*Cant is a useless or trite expression.

his observation of dying patients, said to a pastor's conference, "People who die *for* something are better off than those who die *from* something." He added, "For Christ, His will to live and His will to die were the same."

Our quest must begin with the central Person of history, the Lord Jesus Christ. He announced, "I am the Living One; I was dead, and behold I am alive for ever and ever!" (Rev. 1:18).

What tremendous assurance! Jesus changed the nature of life's final event so that Christians can say, "Where, O death, is your victory? Where, O death, is your sting? . . . Thanks be to God! He gives us the victory through our Lord Jesus Christ" (1 Cor. 15:55, 57).

Yet, even for the Christian, death has power. Paul wrote his friends in Thessalonica so they would not "grieve like the rest of men, who have no hope" (1 Thess. 4:13). But Paul never suggested that Christians would have no sorrow when they are rubbed raw by life's final theft. "The contrast," says Leon Morris, "is not between one degree of sorrow and another, but between Christian hope and pagan despair."[3]

Christians know the emotions James Russell Lowell expressed in his poem "After the Burial," written following the death of his daughter, Rose. Before the poem was completed, his wife also died. Out of the reservoir of his sorrow, he wrote,

> *That little shoe in the corner,*
> *So worn and wrinkled and brown,*
> *With all its emptiness confutes you*
> *And argues your wisdom down.*[4]

Does life have meaning despite death's power? Joe's mother said, "I think I could take this if I knew there would be other children in heaven because of Joe."

Does human life have any value? Or, are we just "dust in the wind," as one cynic has put it?

Jesus spoke clearly to this human longing when He said, "I am the resurrection and the life. He who believes in me will live, even though he dies" (John 11:25).

Human Explanations of the Mystery

In an attempt to explain the mysteries that haunt, and sometimes taunt us, we turn to personal experience. We analyze the events of our lives to see if they will help us understand what happens after life's final event.

Near-death experiences. We are drawn to unexplained and unexplainable human events called "near-death" experiences. Many of these episodes are similar. The individual involved recalls an "out-of-the-body" happening that coincided with what others called death. Often these incidents were accompanied by good feelings, a shining white light, and a general feeling of peace. Then, with some reluctance, the person returned to what we call life.

Some of those who have reported "near-death" experiences are people of such transparent honesty we would never accuse them of lying. Others are so naive they don't have enough finesse to lie convincingly.

However, not all people report good feelings from their "near-death" experience. Their sensations ranged from despair to horror, combined with darkness and fear.

What are we to make of all this? There is only enough here to whet our appetite, but not to give us clear direction for the future.

Sensing the "presence" of the departed. Some people report that they sensed the "presence" of the departed. These events don't follow a pattern, but my father's experience is like that of many people. One Sunday morning a few months following my mother's death, he was overcome with grief. His tears were interrupted by a "sense that Mother was with me." He isn't sure, but thinks he may have seen a vision of her.

Was she there, speaking words of comfort; or did his awareness spring from his own memory? He was never sure. But the moment was so real it helped him turn the corner in his grief. From then on, he reports, he found it easier to adjust to her death.

Common Views About Death and the Afterlife

Whatever these human experiences may mean, we still wonder about the future that confronts us.

Some deny any problem. In his penetrating novel *The Robe*, Lloyd Douglas has this conversation take place between Marcellus, the Roman soldier in charge of Christ's crucifixion, and his slave Demetrius. It begins with Demetrius quoting the Roman philosopher, Lucretius.

"'Lucretius thinks it is the fear of death that makes men miserable,' went on Demetrius, 'he's for abolishing that fear.'

"'A good idea,' argued Marcellus languidly, 'How does he propose to do it?'

"'By assuming that there is no future life,' explained Demetrius.

"'That would do it,' drawled Marcellus—'provided the assumption would stay where you put it.'"[5] His sarcasm points out that simply denying a future life will do nothing to comfort our fears about death and what lies beyond.

A fatalistic view of life and death. Comments about death range widely. One frightened soldier explained his courage by saying, "When a bullet comes with your name on it, you can't dodge it; till then you're safe." The cynical poet Swinburne wrote:

> *From too much love of living,*
> *From hope and fear set free,*
> *We thank with brief thanksgiving*
> *Whatever gods may be*

> *That no life lives forever;*
> *That dead men rise up never;*
> *That even the weariest river*
> *Winds somewhere safe to sea.*[6]

Continued human achievement. Others counter fatalism and denial with the conviction that the future is a place for continued improvement. All forms of reincarnation, from ancient Hinduism to the current New Age movement, fit into this category. So does Robert Browning's couplet from *Andrea del Sarto:*

Ah, but a man's reach should exceed his grasp,
Or what's a heaven for?

We started out by asking, "What does the Christian faith have to say to all those in grief who ask questions about the afterlife?" Specifically, we want to know, "What about the Christian dead?" Let's turn to that question now.

The Christian Dead

This chapter was prompted by these questions: *What is George doing? Does he miss me? Does he ask You about me and the children?* These are poignant questions. Questions of hope, but hope tinged with sadness. The last question carries faith and testimony with it. Had George so followed the Lord Jesus here that he had a reunion with Him over there? That seems to be the strong implication, doesn't it?

We begin with the seemingly obvious conclusion that the widow's questions aren't answered directly in the Bible, or they would not have been asked. Yet, we can start with the Bible to find possible answers for these questions.

The dead are. At first glance this appears to be an incomplete sentence. But, in fact, it is a profound statement that goes to the heart of the New Testament's understanding of life beyond the grave. People, to refute Swinburne's imagery, do not find their destiny by disappearing into nonbeing, like a river swallowed by the sea. Individuality and consciousness continue into the next life.

Actually, this applies to all people, not only the Christian dead. In the story Jesus told, the righteous beggar and the calloused rich man had different destinies, yet both continued as persons in the beyond (Luke 16:19 ff.).

This Christian concept goes contrary to the idea common among Jewish leaders in Jesus' time. With only a few exceptions, the Old Testament is pessimistic concerning the future life. It refers to *Sheol,* the dark land of the forgotten dead. In Ps. 6:5 David says to God, "There is no mention of Thee in death; in Sheol who will give Thee thanks?" (NASB). But the New Testament teaches, the dead are—they continue to exist. "Blessed are the dead who die in the Lord" (Rev. 14:13). In the deepest theological sense, "Life goes on."

The Christian dead are with Jesus. Now we narrow our search for meaning from all people to the "dead in Christ" (1 Thess. 4:16). We begin with Paul's comment about "those who have fallen asleep in [Jesus]" (v. 14).

What does it mean to "fall asleep" in Jesus? Jesus gave those who believe in Him a new view of death. "For pagans death was the end of everything," Leon Morris writes. "But for Christians it was no more than sleep."[7]

Luke used this same phrase to describe the death of Stephen (Acts 7:60). Just before the mob killed him, "Stephen . . . looked up to heaven and saw the glory of God, and Jesus standing at the right hand of God. 'Look,' he said, 'I see heaven open and the Son of Man standing at the right hand of God' . . . While they were stoning him, Stephen prayed, 'Lord Jesus, receive my spirit' . . . When he had said this, *he fell asleep"* (vv. 55-56, 59-60, emphasis added).

Some hold to the opinion that in death souls are sleeping, unconsciously awaiting their resurrection. Most Christians view death as an immediate gateway into the presence of Jesus. Jesus himself told the repentant thief on the cross, *"Today* you will be with me in paradise" (Luke 23:43, emphasis added).

How can we be sure that the Christian dead are with Jesus? Paul wrote, "For to me, to live is Christ and to die is gain. . . . I am torn between the two: *I desire to depart and be with Christ"* (Phil. 1:21, 23, emphasis added).

Jesus is with the Father and invites us to join them.

"I am going there to prepare a place for you," Jesus told His disciples in the Upper Room the night before His death. "And if I go and prepare a place for you, I will come back and take you to be with me" (John 14:2-3).

The Christian dead have a body. The Christians in Corinth were Greeks. The Greeks believed in immortality, but not in the resurrection of the body. But the Christian faith teaches us something entirely different. Jesus had a body after His resurrection. A different body, to be sure, than the one He used building tables and hanging doors in Nazareth, but a body nevertheless.

I can remember Dr. H. Orton Wiley, the great theologian and Bible scholar, replying to the question, "What kind of body will we have after death?"

He said, "I won't know what it will be like until I see Jesus. Then I'll know, for the Bible says, 'We shall be like him, for we shall see him as he is'" (1 John 3:2).

As Paul said, "We will all be changed" (1 Cor. 15:51). Changed into a spiritual body; a glorified body with which to praise the Lord.

The Christian dead are comfortable and freed to worship the Lord without human limitations. A lady in a wheelchair was asked, "Is this a permanent disability? Are you going to be in that wheelchair all your life?"

She replied with a smile, "No, just till I get to heaven."

The apostle Paul exalts that new life in Christ with a series of comparisons. Note the contrasts he makes between this life and the next: perishable—imperishable; dishonor—glory; weakness—power; human genetic structure—heavenly likeness; earthly—heavenly (1 Cor. 15:42-49).

John, in his picture of the future, said this about those who die in Jesus, "Never again will they hunger; never again will they thirst. . . . And God will wipe away every tear from their eyes" (Rev. 7:16-17). Freed from human limitations, Christians will be able to worship the Lord in ways denied them in this life.

The Source of Our Hope

Christ's resurrection guarantees our life—now and eternally. We will be safe in Him. Paul told the Corinthian Christians, "For if the dead are not raised, then Christ has not been raised either. And if Christ has not been raised, your faith is futile . . . *But Christ has indeed been raised from the dead*" (1 Cor. 15:16-17, 20, emphasis added). Our hope in Christ is not useless because His resurrection from the dead has guaranteed our future.

When Christ returns from heaven, "The dead in Christ will rise first. . . . We . . . will be caught up together with them . . . And so we will be with the Lord forever" (1 Thess. 4:16-17). Christ's resurrection assures us that Christians can follow Him to glorious and eternal victory.

But what about George? What's he doing now? Questions like these show us how close we live to the edge of life's mysteries. The teachings of Jesus Christ do not clear up all our earth-bound mysteries. On the contrary, the deepest mysteries of all are found in the death and resurrection of our Lord. Jesus' resurrection opens the door for all Christians to follow.

Antonín Dvořák, the greatest Czech composer of his

time, visited the United States in 1892. Out of his extreme homesickness and his fascination with African American and Native American melodies, Dvořák composed a new symphony. In one section, Dvořák caught the spirit of the "spirituals" with a theme that speaks to our "homesickness for heaven." It captures the mood of Christians who seek for answers and look forward to reunion with friends and loved ones who are already in the presence of Jesus. We close our quest in this chapter with these words, which capture the spirit of Dvořák's symphony, *From the New World:*

> *Goin' home, goin' home, I'm just goin' home;*
> *It's not far, just close by—through an open door.*

One of these days everyone who has accepted Jesus as Lord will walk through that open door to see Him face-to-face. Perhaps we'll meet George too.

Notes

1. C. S. Lewis, *A Grief Observed* (New York: Seabury Press, 1961), 7.
2. Ibid., 60.
3. Leon Morris, *The Epistles of Paul to the Thessalonians* (Leicester, England: InterVarsity Press, 1984), 89.
4. Howard L. Stimmel, *Rendezvous with Eternity* (New York: Abingdon-Cokesbury Press, 1947), 62.
5. Lloyd C. Douglas, *The Robe* (Boston: Houghton Mifflin Co., 1947), 135.
6. Paul S. Rees, *Things Unshakable* (Grand Rapids: Wm. B Eerdmans Publishing Co., 1947), 148.
7. Leon Morris, *The First Epistle of Paul to the Corinthians* (Leicester, England: InterVarsity Press, 1989), 208.

THE UESTION

"Why am I like I am?"

THE SSUES

- Why do I feel like my body is ugly?
- If I'm saved, why can't I overcome my bad habits?
- Why do I have bad attitudes?

BACKGROUND SCRIPTURE:

Rom. 12:1-2

4

What Makes Us What We Are?

by Les Parrott III

WHEN I LOOK in the mirror, I wish I could make a few changes. My chin needs help. My nose is a tad too long. There's a ridge along the back of my head that makes my hair look funny. People think I am too sober when really I am smiling on the inside. It makes me ask, "Why am I like I am?"

A woman in my counseling office put it this way: "My husband likes eating at home. I like eating out. I have a low threshold for pain. He goes to the dentist without flinching. I suppress my strong emotions. He talks things out. He likes everybody. I only have a few close friends. I'm a night owl. He's a morning person. What makes me like [this] when I would like to be more like him? I've tried to change, but I come up being somebody who isn't me. Can God help me to be different without feeling like a phony?"

Dr. Les Parrott III is a professor of psychology and director of the Center for Relationship Development at Seattle Pacific University. His books include *Helping the Struggling Adolescent* (Zondervan) and *Love's Unseen Energy: Overcoming Guilt to Build Healthy Relationships* (Zondervan).

After an evening service at our church, my wife and I met another couple at one of our favorite Seattle restaurants. It's a kind of habit for the four of us to share a snack on Sunday nights. Not long ago we were laughing and talking about superficialities: the rain, the beauty of the lights on Puget Sound, the way the 'Sonics were winning, the way things were going at work. We soon exhausted the superficial subjects, and the conversation became more serious. Someone mentioned the morning sermon, and my friend turned pensive.

"What are you thinking?" I asked.

"If I am born again, why am I so imperfect?" he said.

That question was the catalyst for a discussion that lasted for the rest of the evening. We entered a dialogue. We stayed so long I thought we would have to pay rent on the table. The talk focused on two fundamental questions: *Why am I like I am?* and *How can I change?*

I have given a lot of thought to these questions. So did the apostle Paul. In a flash of psychological and spiritual insight, Paul put his finger squarely on the answers. He wrote to his friends in Rome, "I urge you . . . to offer your bodies as living sacrifices . . . Do not conform any longer to the pattern of this world, but be transformed by the renewing of your mind" (Rom. 12:1-2). I am always amazed at the way Scripture and studies in human nature confirm each other. In this brief paragraph Paul puts his finger on the three factors that constitute the raw material of who we are:

- our biology
- our environment
- our attitude

Presenting Our Bodies

The first factor in the making of who we are is biological. Skin color, size, weight, gender, and physical features are all biological factors over which we have little or no control. But these factors by themselves do not really make us who we are. The way we feel about them is what matters.

For instance, how would I feel about myself if suddenly I were six inches taller? For some people, this additional height would be the beginning of a great new life. For others, it would be pure misery.

Here is the other side of the same question: What if I were suddenly six inches shorter? What would this do to my personality? For many people, a sudden loss of six inches from their stature would be devastating.

Let me ask another question. If it were possible, what color would I choose to be? Would this make any difference in the way I feel about myself and others?

Or what would happen if I were suddenly 50 pounds heavier? Would that make me "jolly"? Not if I had to deal with self-imposed guilt over obesity.

What would happen if each of us could push a magic button and be the age we would like to be, the height we think is most appropriate, the weight we would enjoy, and possess the physical characteristics we consider to be most beautiful or handsome? Would this make any difference in who we are? Without doubt, the results of pushing the magic button would be miraculous, not because of our physical changes, but because of the emotional changes that would accompany them. This is why Paul wrote his Roman friends, "I urge you . . . offer your bodies as living sacrifices, holy and pleasing to God" (Rom. 12:2). People who cannot accept themselves physically often suffer.

Paul's remarks were addressed to many Christians who were slaves. A change in color or nationality would have made a miraculous difference in their lives. But Paul urged them to learn how to accept what they could not change.

The road to inner peace begins by accepting ourselves the way we are—age, color, girth, height—instead of the way we might wish to be. Christians who cannot present themselves to God as acceptable develop a set of attitudes that make their lives difficult.

The Big Squeeze

Another factor that influences who we are is the environment or cultural setting we lived in for the first 12 years of our lives. Even more important is the way we feel about our experiences during those growing-up years. Paul said, "Do not conform any longer to the pattern of this world" (Rom. 12:2). J. B. Phillips translates it, "Don't let the world around you squeeze you into its own mould."

What was life like around the 12th birthday? That is a question that can produce vivid images for most people. Other provocative questions come under the same umbrella. What side of town was our house on—the rich or poor? How often did we move? Where were we in the family birth order? How did our mother and father treat each other?

By the time we can speak the language of the culture into which we are born, we are the victims of it. By the time we can assert our will in the family, we have internalized its eating habits, attitudes, and behavior patterns.

Imagine for a moment, three young adults coming out of three different backgrounds and then meeting on the campus of a Christian college.

One African-American student came from the ghetto of a big city where drugs, guns, and gangs were a way of life. Then he was converted. At the urging of a godly pastor, he went off to a Holiness school.

The second student was raised on the Papago reservation south of Tucson, Arizona. There Native American young people who tried to work in the city were hired last, fired first, and talked about within their hearing as though they were a different species of the human race. At night these youth went home to the poorest of circumstances. In a Holiness church on the reservation, the young person was converted and eventually enrolled in a Christian college.

The third student came from a prosperous, white, middle-class community where growing up in a thriving, evangelical church with many enrichment programs for children and teenagers was taken for granted. Attending a Christian university was assumed from childhood.

When these three saved-and-sanctified young people meet, they are not going to interpret things alike. The differences in their perspectives will be dramatic.

The bottom line: By the time we are 12, the circumstances of our childhood have pushed us into a mold forged from the attitude and behavior patterns of the people whose opinions we valued as a child.

Yet, no one needs to live his or her adult years dominated by a poor self-image that comes only from childhood experiences. We may have been told we were dumb or ugly, but no adult has to live with the same picture of self-worth that was handed to him or her by people who were unworthy to judge in the first place.

For too many, the guilt of sin is gone by the grace of God; but the shame that comes from feelings of inadequacy and fear of failure is crystallized into a self-concept. What a waste to live an adult life emotionally crippled when the saving grace of God can teach us to see who we are in Christ Jesus—redeemed, resurrected, empowered, and loved.

The Divine Transformation

Some things even God doesn't do. God doesn't turn back the calendar to a former era in our lives. God doesn't change the physical factors that endowed our births. We are already female or male, tall or short, big or small, smart or ordinary, agile or clumsy. Some of these factors can be changed slightly within small limits. But basically, God doesn't make tall people short. He doesn't replace arms lost in battle. God doesn't go back and rerun the experiences that conditioned our childhoods. That era of life is over. The chronological calendar is irreversible.

Yet, God can do wonderful things with our spirit if we let Him. Paul said, "Be transformed by the renewing of your mind" (Rom. 12:2). That is how we change who we are—by transforming our mind.

Some people believe a great emotional experience is God's way of transforming persons. Others count on theological truth for changing lives. Still others look to heartwarming worship experiences for periodic spiritual tune-ups. All these ways of spiritual change are worthy. But God's way, according to His Word, is to transform the mind.

To me, the best analogy for the mind is the computer. Every computer has been programmed by someone to function in certain ways according to the signals it receives. The mind receives data from what we see, hear, smell, taste, and touch. However, we also have the capacity to stamp incoming data with a negative or positive impression before it is permanently filed away in the brain. By the time we have reached adulthood, the habit of stamping every experience positive or negative becomes a way of life. It's how our "computer" works.

God does not turn back history. He doesn't wipe out what has happened. But He can help us reprogram our computer so we are changed permanently and completely from within.

In the Christian university where I teach, chapel

speakers and students can gather at a round table in the student center to talk. One old man, who had a better chapel attendance record than some students, always came to the round table although he had no direct connection to the university.

Shortly after birth, Leslie Berge's mother left him in a box on the steps of a Seattle orphanage. He grew up tough. Everything he fed into his computer came up negative, cynical, and critical. Verbal and physical abuse were his weapons of choice.

However, the famous contralto opera star, Madam Schumann-Heink (1862-1936), once visited the orphanage. After singing, she explained how she would like to take someone back to New York with her and asked for volunteers. Leslie Berge shot up his hand. He didn't know anything about New York, and he had never heard of the famous singer. But he would do anything to get out of that orphanage where he was fed poorly and bullied.

Leslie Berge made the cross-country train trip to New York, where he lived in the stylish apartment of the cultured singer. Eventually, he was hired as a waiter by the Waldorf-Astoria Hotel. But he floundered. Things did not go well. He was on his way to being fired when another waiter took him aside and explained what was happening. To shorten the story, Leslie gave his heart to Christ and began the process of deprogramming a set of crippling attitudes that had cast sourness over his entire life. Leslie allowed God to transform his mind.

Students sat transfixed as Mr. Berge, who was the maître d' at the Waldorf-Astoria for 37 years, visited the student discussion table during his retirement years. His stories were compelling and filled with insight.

He dedicated the rest of his years to visiting men in the Snohomish, Washington, County Jail. He reasoned, "I have come to realize that every man in prison was abused emotionally or physically when he was a child. And God can do something about that."

It is not possible to change the biological factor in our lives. Our early environment cannot be changed either. But one thing can be changed—our minds can be transformed.

THE QUESTION

"Why has alcoholism taken my husband's heart and mind? Is there really hope for my husband to be back with the children and me?"

THE ISSUES

- Am I really powerless to overcome bad relationships?
- Why isn't the church helping me or my husband?
- Does God really love me?

BACKGROUND SCRIPTURE:

Pss. 18; 131; 139:23-24; Luke 24:39; John 20:27; Rom. 7:15; 8:26-27; 12:9-21; 15:1-5; 2 Cor. 5:17; Phil. 4:4-9; James 1:2-4; 1 John 2:28

5

Where Is God in Addiction?

by Paul Fitzgerald

S HERRI* GLANCED at her watch. She was surprised that her group had been meeting for more than an hour. Her fear that nobody would understand her story was gone. She had questioned if anyone could understand what she had been through. Now she sensed that this was the right place for her. The group respected her silence. Most had been coming only a few months and recalled their fear in that first meeting.

June continued her response to the question, "The last time you encountered an angry or critical person (e.g., spouse, boss, friend), how did you find yourself reacting?" She experienced overwhelming fear whenever her husband exploded in a rage in front of the children. His compulsive pattern of anger with authority figures had led to trouble at work again. They had moved from their hometown where he had lost several jobs over his rage. She was afraid it was happening all over again.

Dr. Paul Fitzgerald is a counselor and pastor in Somerset, Kentucky, and specializes in working with Christian recovery groups.

Bob shared about his fear of facing his wife in their first family session at the hospital where she was in addiction treatment. A nurse, she struggled with addiction to prescription drugs. She had tried to stop on her own, but it never lasted long. Life had finally become unbearable for Bob and their teenage children. He had arranged with a therapist, their pastor, and the few friends for an intervention. Together, they had confronted her with specific incidents where her addictive behavior had hurt them. She had agreed to be admitted for treatment but angrily told Bob she felt abandoned and betrayed. Bob was not sure she would ever want to see him again.

Sherri heard other members share how afraid they were of alcoholic spouses who threatened them. She recognized the stories so similar to her own. Her unconscious nodding became a rocking motion of her whole body. She began sobbing quietly, and the group waited in silence. She pulled a tissue from her purse. "I'm sorry. I really didn't mean to cry like this."

June spoke up immediately, "That's all right, honey. In this group it's safe to feel anything. You can tell us as much or as little as you want."

Sherri responded to the opening and told them how afraid she had been to come to the meeting. "I have prayed to God for years to help pull my husband out of alcoholism, but it has only gotten worse. My sister keeps telling me to leave him, but I haven't been able to do that. I am his only connection to the church. Where is God in all this mess?"

The group was nodding in recognition of her story. They had lived through similar experiences and had asked the same questions: How can you help an addicted spouse? What does a Christian do to help an addicted spouse? What can the church do to help us? Does God really love me?

Anxious Responses to Addiction

Ask the spouse of someone addicted to alcohol, drugs, work, spending, gambling, food, sex, etc., and they can name what does not work. They have tried pretending that the problem was not addiction. They have covered up and made excuses, hoping it would go away. They have taken on the full responsibility for the household and family. They have tried to control the finances and have tried being constantly with the addict to control their choices. They have nagged, threatened, yelled at them, hidden money, cried, and threatened to leave. Over time, these efforts take a toll emotionally and spiritually. They become exhausted, depressed, and despair of finding any help. It seems that even God has abandoned them.

These are just a few of the anxious responses to the anxiety presented by their spouses' addictive choices. Addictions have complex physical, emotional, and spiritual causes. Addictive use of a substance or a process (e.g., gambling, spending) begins as a way of coping with problems that seem overwhelming. The relief is temporary, but the result is increased anxiety that is brought home and dumped on the family. The family's anxious response to their behavior confirms the addict's fears. A vicious cycle of increasingly anxious responses begins, which can quickly reach the point of explosion. A habitual communication pattern develops in which each person comes to know where the anxious exchanges will end, even before it begins. Everyone is doing something, but none of it leads to recovery.

Emotional and Physical Cutoff Response to Addiction

An alternative response to the stress of life with an addict is an emotional and physical cutoff of contact with the addict. After all the anxious responses have failed, a cutoff may seem to be the only option left. The family becomes emotionally exhausted. The thought of more efforts to change the addict and the fear of failure are overwhelming. Spouses feel driven to an emotional and physical cutoff when their anger and exhaustion exceeds their fear of being alone.

Leaving the addict's physical presence because of physical, emotional, or sexual abuse is always an appropriate choice. Everyone has the right to protection from abusive behavior. Children must be protected from the risk of abuse. In the absence of abuse, a spouse may suddenly switch from anxious responses to a cutoff of emotional or physical presence as self-protection from the addict's anxiety. A cutoff may provide an immediate escape for the family, but it usually leaves the addict more anxious and feeling abandoned. Relief for the family may be short-lived as well. New challenges and choices must be faced for which they may be emotionally, physically, and spiritually unprepared.

The Response of Nonanxious Emotional Presence

Remaining emotionally present yet choosing nonanxious responses to the addict's behavior is challenging. The support of others who have been through similar experiences is critical to avoid falling back into anxious responses or cutoffs as the addiction worsens. This response requires finding a healthy spirituality that affirms the dignity of choice for the addict's family members, puts responsibility on the addict to choose whether or not to pursue recovery, and recognizes God at work in the painful process. Following are the steps to adopting the response of nonanxious emotional presence.

Accept That the Problem Exists

It is usually difficult for family and friends to accept that the term "addict" describes the compulsive behaviors of a loved one. The person may be effectively functioning in some areas of life, while failing in others. Forget the stereotype of an addict as someone lying in a gutter. Addicts more often than not look like everyone else.

The addicted person is the last one to accept that a problem exists. His or her defense mechanism of denial appears as obvious lying to everyone else, but it allows the addict to not see what would be too painful to admit. Addicts learn to evade any mention of the addiction and problems resulting from their choices. They shift the focus to other people and problems that become the "real reason" for their problems. They shift blame outside themselves for their addictive choices.

Adults and children who live with an addict are negatively affected by that relationship. The addict's ability to deny that their problem exists or to shift the blame, often to the spouse, may be so effective that others accept blame. Life with an addict has been described as "crazy-making." Obviously painful behavior is denied as if it did not exist. Family members may come to doubt their own sanity. The effects of living with an addict can be very serious, requiring a recovery process separate from the addict's recovery. The term most often used to describe the result of living with an addict is "codependency."

Acceptance that the problem exists is the first step in helping the addict. The family's admission of the problem cannot wait on the addict's acceptance that the problem exists. Acceptance requires breaking free of the denial and blaming used by the addict. It requires breaking the silence and talking to someone about the experience of living with the addict. The goal is not to find someone to fix the problem but to find others with whom reality can be tested to avoid being pulled back into denial. Hopefully, it will be possible to talk confidentially to a pastor knowledgeable about addictions who will encourage and support the recovery process.

Educate Yourself About Addiction

If a spouse or child was diagnosed with a rare disease, most of us would ask questions and go to the library to find out all we could about the condition and how to treat it. The same approach holds for addictions. There are many myths about addiction that are widely accepted but have no basis in reality. In recent years, helpful books on addiction and the effects of living with an addict are easily found, even in Christian bookstores.

Libraries have references for national organizations for recovery of specific addictions (e.g., Alcoholics Anonymous, Overeaters Anonymous, Gamblers Anonymous) that offer toll-free numbers to call for free literature. They also have lists of local chapters in most communities that offer information and support. In the last decade, many churches have begun recovery ministries that offer information and support in the context of the church. (The National Association for Christian Recovery is a fellowship of Christians who identify themselves as being in recovery and maintain a national directory of clergy and counselors knowledgeable about recovery.)

Take the Steps of Healthy Spiritual Surrender

Recovery from addictions and from the effects of living with an addict is at its heart a spiritual process. There are many examples where the cycle of addiction has been immediately broken in a crisis spiritual experience. More often, recovery requires a spiritually healing process in addition to a single crisis experience.

The Twelve Steps of Alcoholics Anonymous has proven to be one effective tool for the process of recovery. The steps can and have been adapted into a specifically

Christian context to counter many kinds of addictions and compulsive behaviors. Here we have presented an adaptation of the first three steps, suggesting how the addict's spouse may begin the process of recovery.

Step One—"We admitted we were powerless over our addicted loved one—that our lives had become unmanageable." This step requires acceptance that no one can change another who does not want to change. It also requires honesty about the consequences of living with an addict. As addictions progressively worsen over time, the chaos felt by family and friends increases. This is not giving up on the addict, but it is giving up on trying to be powerful enough to change him or her. It accepts our "powerlessness over" the choices of others yet does not deny our responsibility of making healthy choices in our situation.

Step Two—"Came to believe that God could restore us to sanity." This step implies that past choices have not been in the best interest of ourselves or our loved ones. Acknowledging that may feel strange, since we have tried to do the best we knew. Often there is a pattern of doing the same things over and over, expecting but not seeing the desired results.

This step shows clearly that the move from addiction to recovery must be a God-directed process. Where we are weak and ineffective to conquer addictions, God is adequate, willing, and already working to restore individuals and families to a state of relationship with Him and with each other.

Step Three—"Made a decision to turn our will and our lives over to the care of God." This is often the first step claimed by both the addict and the spouse when things are at their worst. Sometimes it seems as though the decision is taken back when things improve. The challenge of this step is to really leave the results of turning over life and will to God. We all are ready at times to turn over life when it seems out of control, but we turn it over assuming it will turn out the way we want. Admitting our "powerlessness over" in the first step prepares for this step and truly letting go of the results to God. Recovery cannot be truly effective without acknowledging our weakness, our sinfulness, our repentance, our faith, and most of all His grace.

These are basic steps in a spiritual formation process that embraces God as both emotionally present and a source of nonanxiety. Scripture suggests that God desires an emotionally intimate relationship with His people (e.g., Pss. 131; 139). Other passages identify God as being like a nonanxious Rock, Strong Tower, and Fortress for His people (e.g., Pss. 18; 31; 62). Jesus' teaching in the Sermon on the Mount centers on God's strength and stability becoming the source of the ability to make nonanxious choices in anxious situations. Rom. 12:9-21; 15:1-5; and Phil. 4:4-9 are just a few examples where believers are challenged to make nonanxious choices. Both Rom. 8:26-28 and James 1:2-4 proclaim that God is actively involved in the lives of people through both pleasant and painful experiences to reveal His will for their character development.

Seek the Support You Need

Contact your pastor or a Christian mental health professional to evaluate the possibility of an intervention. Addictions progressively require more and more use of the addictive substance or process to provide similar levels of relief. Over time the addict's health diminishes, family finances become strained, and relationships begin to die. To maintain denial, the addict isolates more and more from those who would tell how they are being hurt. Given enough time, the addict deteriorates and "hits bottom" where denial is finally broken by enough pain. At the bottom, addicts have three choices: die, break mentally, or make the choice to seek God and to enter the recovery process.

Rather than waiting for the natural progression of addiction, the addict's family and friends may be able to intervene. An intervention should only be undertaken with the guidance of an experienced counselor and requires that all family agree to involve themselves in the intervention process.

Find others who have had similar experiences with an addicted spouse. Like Sherri, the addict's spouse assumes that no one has had quite the same experience. Shame keeps us from telling anyone how we are suffering. Fear that others would abandon us if they found out keeps us silent and stuck. Ideally, your church would have a support group to provide the needed emotional and spiritual encouragement.

Confidentially share your situation with your pastor and other spiritual friends. Ask them for their prayer support as you seek wisdom in making nonanxious choices. Prayer is the greatest asset the church and believers have, yet it may be the most underappreciated. The burden of this group may expand to others in similar situations and shape new directions in ministry for the church.

One of every 10 adults in the United States is an alcoholic (2 out of 100 people in Canada). Each alcoholic negatively affects the lives of 4 to 6 others. An estimated 30 million Americans are adult children of alcoholics and struggle with the effects of growing up in an alcoholic family. Estimates are that as many as 5.5 million born-again believers grew up in alcoholic families.[1] Add other addictions and the negative effects of dysfunctional family environments and the population affected is staggering. An unrecognized number of people in the pews of churches each week have been affected by addiction and similar dysfunctional situations. The church can hardly ignore the challenge of presenting the grace of God in ways that address the spiritual formation needs of this population.

In recognition of this challenge, the number of churches sponsoring support group ministries has dramatically increased. Support groups do not have the same purpose as Bible studies, prayer groups, sharing groups, or group therapy, although they may experience each of these elements. Bill Morris defines a church-based support group as "a fellowship of people who come together to share our common experience, strength, and hope with one another so that we can identify our struggles, learn about life and relationships, and grow in the ability to trust God and become all that He created us to be."[2]

He identifies the link between a support group and the biblical concept of the church as a *koinonia* group in six characteristics: honesty, acceptance, respect, openness, encouragement, and responsibility. Support groups provide vital opportunities to minister to the needs of many who might not otherwise seek help from the church. They also provide a valuable opportunity for those who found support and hope to minister to others.

Addiction, codependency, and dysfunctional issues all call for a response from the Christian community. What a marvelous and unique opportunity to proclaim the grace of God that goes beyond the power of our wrong choices, beyond our weaknesses, beyond our shame to offer us hope and a better way to live in relationship with those around us. In God's power and unfailing love, we can choose to reflect the holiness of character that God calls each of us to live.

NOTES

*All names have been changed.

1. Sandra D. Wilson, *Counseling Adult Children of Alcoholics*, ed. Gary R. Collins, Resources for Christian Counseling, Vol. 21 (Dallas: Word, 1989), xii.

2. Bill Morris, *The Complete Handbook for Recovery Ministry in the Church* (Nashville: Thomas Nelson, 1993).

THE QUESTION

"How should I prioritize my time to help my children establish lifelong Christian values?"

THE ISSUES

- I feel too busy to do everything I need to do.
- I've seen other children fail to adopt Christian values and that scares me.
- I feel responsible yet inadequate to guide my children's development.

BACKGROUND SCRIPTURE:

Matt. 6:19-34; 22:36-39

6

This Schedule's Killing Us!

by Bonnie Perry

MOM, can you lie here and talk to me? Just the two of us?"

It was the third time in three weeks 12-year-old Sarah had asked me the question. I would have to say no again tonight. As I hesitated, she grabbed my hand. "For a long time, Mom. Just the two of us. Please?"

I dropped my head, closed my eyes, and sighed. I could hear the echoes of a good friend's advice, "Do it now, Bonnie. In a few years she won't be asking you."

I really wanted to, but I'd worked all day and was so tired. It was already 30 minutes past Sarah's bedtime. Though tomorrow was Saturday, she had to be up at 8:00 to play soccer. I could hear one of my other three children calling me. "Mom! C'mere, Mom! Mooomm! Mom, hurry up."

Bonnie Perry, a freelance writer, lives in Greenwood, Missouri, with her husband and four children. She recently changed jobs so she could spend more time with her family.

Quickly I squeezed Sarah's hand. "I will . . . soon. I promise. But it's too late tonight, and we have such a busy day tomorrow. Don't give up on me, OK?" I rumpled her hair, kissed her forehead, and left the room feeling miserable and guilty.

How had our lives come to this? I asked myself. I'd read all the Christian psychologists' books on parenting. My husband and I knew the dangers of becoming too busy. Yet here we were—juggling two careers, four children, innumerable athletic events, piano practices, and church activities. I hated the fact I was actually having to *schedule* time to spend with my kids.

Does the dilemma sound familiar? To some degree, in one form or another, most of us have struggled with it. We would say family is right there at the top of our priority list, second only to our relationship with God. Yet, when we closely examine the daily routine of our lives (who has time to do that?), we must admit that our family gets what little is left of our time, energy, and affection after a long list of obligations is fulfilled.

So what is the answer? How can we prioritize our time to grow emotionally healthy children who have Christian values that will last a lifetime?

For busy families, the first step to reordering priorities is to reevaluate our children's needs. The results may surprise us.

Stability

Many parents take this basic need of children for granted. We think it means providing parents (in our case, two) who love and nurture, a nice house, and food on the table. If those items are in place, we assume our child has a stable environment, at least in comparison with many other children in today's fragmented society.

But for children, the need for stability goes deeper

than the traditional outward fixtures. They live in a difficult and dangerous world. In his book *Stress and Your Child*, psychologist Archibald Hart describes it this way, "For most children today, stress is a fact of life. Expectations are greater. The pressure to grow up is more intense. The competition for success and even for necessities is fierce, and kids are constantly having to prepare for new roles. More and more children . . . attend overcrowded, often dangerous schools, and grow up in a paradoxical society where kids seem to make their own rules and yet are not valued."*

A great deal of the negative stimulation just described comes from outside the family. As parents, we may recognize these stress points, but we feel helpless to alleviate them. Yet, we can take concrete actions to minimize the threat they pose to development and emotional stability.

Give Kids a Place to Be

By "place" I mean an emotional place, not just a physical one. In a large family it may not be possible to furnish children separate rooms. It wouldn't matter anyway if they are never home to enjoy the privacy. Provide instead the luxury of unscheduled time to cultivate personal emotional health. Time to *be*. Be happy. Be sad. Be quiet. Be alone. Be imaginative. Be whomever they wish—with no pressure and no obligations.

Give them *time*. Time to think. Time to laugh. Time to cry. Time to pretend. Time to grow up. Time to _____ (fill in the blank). The verbs—and the possibilities for our children—are endless.

It sounds good, doesn't it? Deciding to try it could bring some resistance from the same ones it would help. Even though it's essential to their emotional health, children may not know how to *be*. If they are like mine were, they are probably too busy playing soccer, practicing the piano, or sitting in front of video games. They may regard eliminating some of these activities as an unwelcome sacrifice. As parents, our role in changing their minds brings me to the next point.

Give Kids Our Time

Notice I didn't say, "Give kids time." I said, "Give kids *our* time." When families overextend with too many events, those activities can begin to perform a baby-sitting function. Dropping a child at gymnastics may give Mom an hour for grocery shopping. Turning on the computer games may be a vehicle for Dad to get some peace and quiet.

Making changes to build stability and peace into a child's stressed-out world will require parents to proceed carefully. Our son James was 10 years old and well into a career with a soccer club when Rex and I made the decision to streamline our lifestyle. His three practices and two games each week would not fit into the new plan. Soccer would have to go. But what about James? Running roughshod over his feelings certainly wasn't an acceptable alternative. Though we knew the decision was best for him, we knew he wouldn't buy into our plan to simplify. He loved to play ball, and five times a week was no burden to him.

Our daughter, Sarah, expressed similar feelings when Rex convened a family meeting to discuss our proposal. She enjoys music and was taking lessons on the piano and the violin. Though she readily admitted that trying to learn two instruments afforded her little time to practice either one, she wasn't sure she wanted to choose. She regarded the whole idea as a tremendous sacrifice.

Eliminating stressors and giving our kids a place to be wasn't an easy decision at our house, although we were able to come to a family consensus. To make it work would require a sacrifice and time commitment from the whole family. For Rex, it meant playing board games when he would rather read the sports page. For me, it meant not caring that we're having a popcorn party on the freshly vacuumed carpet when there are three loads of laundry upstairs waiting to be folded. As parents, we've worked hard to implement positive change and to teach our kids the pleasures of just "hanging out together." Initially, it was tough and took a lot of *our* time. Most of their friends were still involved in multiple activities and were seldom available to play.

Eventually, our time investment paid off; and we won them over. James built a tree house in his spare time. Sarah is learning to cook. Elizabeth, age eight, has decided it's fun to read long books. Joanna, a kindergartner, jumps on our bed every Saturday morning during the school year asking excitedly, "Is it stay-home day, Mama?" With our help, the kids are discovering all kinds of interesting things about their world, mostly things they didn't have the time to think about before. In the process the members of our family are rediscovering one another.

Give Kids Our Personal Best

We've already seen that reprioritizing has to start with parents. Never mind the old adage—quantity really is no substitute for quality. The time we give our children isn't worth much if we're preoccupied with problems at work or wishing we were getting more accomplished elsewhere.

Lifelong Christian values are founded on the familiar words of Jesus we read in Matt. 22:37-39: "'Love the Lord your God with all your heart and with all your soul and with all your mind.' This is the first and greatest commandment. And the second is like it: 'Love your neighbor as yourself.'"

Building lasting values and godly character into our lives boils down to a premise that can be drawn from Jesus' words: People are more important than things. Our families are more important than our careers. But if we are constantly giving our family the leftovers of our time, energy, and attention, we probably are not modeling the same message we are speaking. Our children deserve our personal best. Their self-esteem depends on it, and no amount of things or activities will substitute for it.

If it's true that our family gets what's left of us at the end of the workday, the importance of carefully reprioritizing takes on importance. I suggest, instead of starting small, start big.

As we take stock of our lifestyle, make a list of every outside activity that demands time, energy, or attention. Include job, church commitments, community activities—all "extracurricular" activities. Maybe eliminating a few soccer practices and some voice lessons will solve the problem. I discovered in our situation that eliminating those activities would only put a very small Band-Aid on a very large sore. In that case, consider some creative and radical alternatives.

Do both parents work outside the home? If so, discuss the reasons honestly. If both incomes are necessary to maintain existence, then so be it. If both incomes are needed only to maintain a comfortable existence (however "comfortable" is defined), then reevaluate. Could one parent resign to stay home? Work part time? Job share? Work at home? Change occupations?

As the options are discussed, weigh the implications carefully. It might mean a move to a smaller home. Driving a less expensive car. Selling the boat. Postponing a vacation. Giving up fast food. Review the possibilities and ramifications in each choice. In the process, ask the question, "Am I engaging in this activity because it provides me temporal benefit or because it is eternally significant?"

That Nagging Question

We have talked at great length now about the importance of evaluating our schedules in light of the priority of our children. There is much we can do to create and maintain healthy schedules that give our children a chance to grow and develop in appropriate ways.

However, there remains that plaguing question that lurks in the recesses of every parent's mind. What if, after all I have done to encourage my child's development in relationship to both God and to fellow persons, my child rejects the faith I hold so dearly?

While the wisdom of Proverbs suggests that a child properly trained during early years will not forget that leading in later life, we know from experience that children in godly, properly prioritized families sometimes go astray. What can a parent do when the heartache of a wayward, rebellious child finds an unwelcome room in our home?

The simple, yet difficult to accept, answer is this: A parent can do only so much to influence a child toward God and a healthy view toward life. A positive, well-balanced, spiritually sensitive home environment can give our children many opportunities to make good decisions. Yet each person, each child, ultimately must choose the path that he or she will walk. With that important truth in mind, we as parents and caring adults continue to give full attention to those children who are in our care, trusting that our influence will find a permanent home in their hearts by the power of God's Holy Spirit.

It's Worth It

Rex and I discovered that reprioritizing our lives with our children's eternal well-being in mind has been one of the most significant milestones in our lives. In the process, we have rediscovered that no sacrifice of time, energy, or frills is too great to ensure the proper nurturing of our eternally significant children. As we trust God to help our inadequacies, we have confidence that He takes our meager resources and multiplies them in ways unimaginable. God, the One who modeled the love and care of true parenthood, leads the way for us earthly parents.

I slept on Sarah's floor in a sleeping bag recently. Long after the light was out, we talked about really important stuff—like when she might get her braces off and why there weren't any cute boys in her class.

We fell asleep holding hands.

NOTES

*Archibald D. Hart, *Stress and Your Child* (Dallas: Word Publishing, 1992), vii.

THE QUESTION

"How do I guide a friend who is going astray, without losing him as a friend?"

THE ISSUES

- How can I speak the truth when I am frightened by angry confrontations?
- Wouldn't just praying for my friend be more spiritual—and easier?
- What responsibility do I have for the spiritual development of other Christians?

BACKGROUND SCRIPTURE:

Matt. 5:13-16; 1 Cor. 5:5; Rev. 22:17

7

Should I Speak Up?

by Ed Robinson

I WAS AT THE LOCAL restaurant for my usual meeting with Bob and James. We met every Monday morning to talk about a variety of topics like family, business, politics, and faith. Bob was seated across the table from me. The usually vibrant conversation was labored that morning. James and I were struggling to know what to say to Bob.

He hadn't been there for a few weeks, but I figured that his schedule was crowded. So he had to give up a few appointments, and the Monday meeting was one of them. We'd missed him but hadn't thought much about it; that is, until we heard from a mutual friend that he was separating from his wife after 10 years of marriage. We didn't even know they were having trouble! We didn't know that he'd moved out and was living alone in a studio apartment. We just didn't know. We didn't know what to do either. He was sitting right across the table, and we didn't know how to respond.

What should we say? How should we handle the embarrassment and anger of not knowing something so im-

---

Dr. Ed Robinson is a professor of Christian education at Nazarene Theological Seminary, Kansas City.

portant about a person whom we considered a friend? How deeply should we probe to find out what the problem is? Or is there some way we can offer help or advice? Do we even have the right to "poke our noses" into his personal life? Are we making spiritual judgments about Bob that we have no right to make? If we decide to talk about the issue straight on, do we run the risk of alienating Bob and cutting off the conversation—and friendship—forever? These questions swept over my mind that Monday morning.

I wish I could tell you that I dealt with all the questions adequately that day over 15 years ago. I wish I could —but I can't. I chose to hold back and talk about the less important concerns of the situation and save my most sincere thoughts for my prayers on Bob's behalf. I walked away from that restaurant feeling confused, ineffective, and defeated. I felt like I gave less than my best to a friend.

I've given a lot of thought to that situation and ones like it. The questions accompanying these dilemmas aren't easy, but they're worth addressing.

Out of the questions some basic guidelines emerged to help when I'm faced with the challenge of talking honestly to a friend. I thought of several ways I can proceed around some controversial issue or action in his or her life, especially knowing that the conversation has the potential for negatively impacting our relationship. The ideas aren't all that profound, but they are a guide to giving counsel.

Praying for a Friend

Praying for a friend in need of counsel and direction is never wrong. It sounds too simple to mention. The decision about confronting a friend is never choosing whether we should pray *or* have a direct conversation, but deciding whether to talk *as well as* pray. In fact, prayer is always the place to begin. Seeking God's perspective helps to clarify our assessment of the situation. Prayer enables us to determine whether our friend's action disturbs us because it has potential for destructive results *or* simply because he or she doesn't measure up to our personal preferences. God's perspective should be our ultimate purpose, and our personal motive, in guiding a friend who's going astray.

Prayer can also help us gain the courage to confront, especially if confrontation is difficult for us. Prayer gives the assurance that we never give guidance alone. We are always in the company of the ultimate, confronting guide, the Holy Spirit.

The Christian Community

Within the Christian community, lovingly confronting wrong is not a right—it's a responsibility. For some reason, many have bought into the rugged individualism that characterizes our modern culture. That individualism has some economic and educational benefits but has proved to be disastrous for the social and religious arenas.

Issues of morality and the heart have been placed in the seemingly "off limits" zone of the individual. Things that are most important—that is, most personal—are really "nobody else's business." What a disaster! As Christians, we shy away from lovingly getting involved in other people's problems because we feel we don't have the right. As Christians, we are responsible for each other. We must learn to overcome our hesitancy to graciously engage ourselves in somebody else's "personal business" and seek to be the salt and light we are called to be (see Matt. 5:13-16). What real friend would stand idly by while awful circumstances, bad choices, or sinful behavior wreak havoc in another's life?

Christian Confrontation

Christians always confront with the primary purpose of redemption, reconciliation, and restoration—never condemnation. Something about human nature relishes the opportunity to be right, to win, to have the upper hand. We enjoy being in that powerful position. Confrontation carries all of those temptations. If we can prove another wrong, then we somehow show ourselves to be right or "righteous." Determining our motives in confrontation is essential.

As we point out inconsistencies or challenge sinful actions, our hearts must be full of the same grace that was extended to us when God's Spirit lovingly confronted us and called us to repentance. The final word of judgment from Israel's prophets was always one of invitation to restoration and reconciliation. In his letter to the Corinthians, Paul confronts a problem of immorality by advising them to deal with an immoral brother in their midst so that "his spirit [may be] saved on the day of the Lord" (1 Cor. 5:5). At the end of Revelation, following the description of those who will be inside the city gates and those who will be on the outside, the final image of Christ is one with outstretched arms who announces, "Whoever is thirsty, let him come; and whoever wishes, let him take the free gift of the water of life" (Rev. 22:17). God's motive in confrontation is always redemptive. Ours must be as well.

Advice

Advice is best received in the context of an existing relationship. This is an age of "experts" and "specialists." The morning news/talk shows are stocked with resident health-care experts, consumer advocates, psychological therapists, global political analysts, educational gurus, ad nauseam. Whenever an issue arises about which there may be some disagreement, the network producers cart out the resident "expert" to interpret the validity of a particular study or position.

However, once the pronouncement is made, the opposition produces its own expert to refute the network's judgment. In the process, the uninformed viewer's confusion is increased rather than relieved. So much for the power of experts!

Frankly, most of us don't qualify as an expert in anything. We merely have a decent dose of common sense and can discern good choices from poor ones. Most advice that's given between friends doesn't require the expertise of advanced education, exclusive information, or prior experience. It only requires the validity of an authentic, clear-thinking, loving concern of one friend for another.

The validity of a life lived well is the highest credential one needs to offer a well-timed word of guidance or encouragement. Time and consistent relationship are the two ingredients by which others may know the stability of our lives. This consistency of relationship is sometimes called "earning the right to be heard" or "paying the price to give advice." Whatever we call it, it means backing up the truth of our advice with the long-term character of trustworthiness of our lives. Guidance from a trusted friend, whose motives are unquestionably good, is better received than words from a stranger.

Making a Commitment

Never offer guidance to a friend who's going astray without also making a commitment to be a part of the reconciliation or restoration. We all love a quick fix—a word of advice spoken, a plan activated, a solution reached. Quick, easy, no pain. "As easy as one-two-three." "All's well that ends well." Sounds nice, doesn't it? But it's not realistic. We know that real resolutions to life's problems aren't worked out that neatly. Most require hard choices, great courage, and perseverance. Such factors come much more readily in the context of a community of encouragers. Such factors require a commitment from the community. Any parent who has ever disciplined a child knows that parental responsibility increases rather than decreases during and following the discipline.

Most effective groups are dependent on this principle of personal resolve combined with group accountability and encouragement. A "great cloud of witnesses" can have an amazing effect on one who is struggling to make the right choices and follow through with the appropriate behaviors. Giving advice to a friend who is needing to make some changes in life really is no different. If we offer the advice to change, we must also offer a supportive environment in which the change can take place.

A word of caution. Many well-intentioned Christians have a rescuer's complex. Their main goal is to rescue people from bad situations. The goal is worthy, but it has potential snares. The temptation for the rescuer is to rush in to take charge, relieving the one in distress from any responsibility for initiating change. Rescuers cannot make another person's choices. Rescuers cannot take responsibility for another person's behaviors. Rescuers really do not help much if they simply make others dependent on them. Such dependency perpetuates the problem rather than being its ultimate solution.

When we attempt to give guidance to a friend who's making poor choices, we must offer a sense of direction *and* a supportive friendship that comes alongside for accountability. Such assistance empowers a friend toward lasting change rather than prolonged avoidance of decision and responsibility.

Rejection

We must always be prepared for rejection. As much as we'd like to guarantee that our advice will be received well and our friendship maintained, such an assurance does not exist. As long as people are free to make their own choices, rejection will always be possible. Depending on the severity and urgency of the issue, we may need to place our friendship in jeopardy for the higher value of salvaging a person's moral and spiritual welfare. In many situations where there is a fundamental disagreement of perspectives and values, the quality of friendship may already be deteriorating. In these cases, nonintervention only delays the inevitable.

How do we give advice to a friend who's making some poor moral choices, without threatening the friendship? If we confront lovingly, will we be received or rejected? How hard can we press at the problem without driving a friend away instead of bringing the friend closer? Can't we just love him or her back into an acceptable lifestyle without verbally confronting the wrong? If we do nothing, do we run the risk of watching a person self-destruct and lose the friendship anyway? These are the questions with which we began. We have come full-cycle, and still the tough questions remain.

We can deal with the tough question in one of three ways: (1) Ignore the issue and pray that someone else will deal with it; (2) Take the role of intercessor but choose not to become personally involved in the situation; or (3) Take the role of intervener and choose to involve ourselves in the lives of others with gracious confrontation, steady support, and redeeming reconciliation.

The first option is always wrong. Some choose it and usually become desensitized in the process. The second is sometimes the right way—usually chosen because it's the most comfortable or because an issue is so complex that professional assistance is appropriate. The third is often right. More of us need to choose it with greater regularity. If we would, we might not get stuck talking about trivial matters when a friend in need of counsel sits across the table at the local restaurant.

Should we speak up? Yes, speak up in all the love and prayer we can give.

THE **Q**UESTION

"What is the unpardonable sin?"

THE **I**SSUES

- Have I committed the unpardonable sin?
- Can I commit it without knowing I have?
- Will I be eternally condemned if I didn't mean to commit it?

BACKGROUND SCRIPTURE:

> Mark 3:22-30 (Matt. 12:22-32; Luke 12:10);
> 1 Sam. 16:14; 1 John 1:9

8

The Good News of the Unpardonable Sin

by Carl Leth

I LISTENED with deepening horror. As the preacher vividly described the woman's anguished weeping, I could almost see her sobbing in despair, lying across the altar. Despite her cries for mercy, none came. She had, the preacher explained, declined to respond to the altar call once too often. Now God had withdrawn, leaving her to her despair. She had committed the "unpardonable" sin. She was beyond hope. With that piercing picture before us, the altar invitation was extended.

I have never forgotten that frightening story. Nor did I forget that the same fate could await me. I worried that I might foolishly say the wrong thing. Every altar invitation was a reminder that I could, at any moment, "cross the line." I was haunted by the fear that I could unknowingly pass the reach of God's forgiveness. Despite my earnest—if

---

Dr. Carl Leth is senior pastor of the North Raleigh Church of the Nazarene, Raleigh, North Carolina. He is an avid fan of the basketball team at Duke University, where he earned his Ph.D. in church history.

feeble—attempts to live the Christian life, I was afraid that I would not measure up. Somewhere, at some time, God would give up on me. Then I, too, would be beyond hope.

To my relief, I have learned that my fears were both common and unfounded. The issue of the unpardonable sin has often troubled sincere people. Sadly, it is sometimes treated in ways that are destructive. Let's look together at this issue. There may be some good news here.

When Have I Gone Too Far?

Fear of the finally broken relationship is a common human experience. Lingering nervously in the background of every relationship is the question, "How far can this go?" When and where will we reach the point that is "too far"?

Mary* reached that point when she realized that her husband, Bill*, would never be a success. Joe* and Phyllis* reached that point when Joe finally got tired of struggling with his wife's psychological problems. Sue's* father crossed that point when she came home pregnant. Roger's* employer reached that point when Roger made one too many mistakes managing his inventory.

Even Jesus' disciples wanted an answer to a similar question, "How many times do we have to forgive?" In other words, where do we draw the line? How far do we have to go?

The same question shadows our relationship with God. Jesus raises the question when He speaks of the unpardonable or eternal sin. The key passage is found in Mark 3:22-30 (also recorded in Matt. 12:22-32 and Luke 12:10). In it Jesus responds to the accusations of the teachers of the Law. Jesus concludes His rebuttal with this statement and warning: "I tell you the truth, all the sins and blasphemies of men will be forgiven them. But whoever blasphemes against the Holy Spirit will never be forgiven; he is guilty of an eternal sin" (Mark 3:28-29). If we can learn what this text is teaching us, we can better understand the message of the unpardonable sin.

A State of the Heart

The first lesson is that the unpardonable sin is a state of the heart rather than a specific action. There is broad agreement among commentators that Jesus was not merely condemning an instance of verbal blasphemy by the teachers of the Law. It was really the condition of their hearts that prompted His condemnation. Their judgment had become so twisted that they could look at good and see evil. Their hearts were so hardened that they were no longer moved by evidence of God's presence.

The Holy Spirit makes us sensitive to spiritual things. The Holy Spirit prompts regret for our sinful actions. It is the Holy Spirit who causes dissatisfaction with a life separated from God. The Holy Spirit whispers to the prodigal reminders of home and a loving father. It is the work of the Holy Spirit to bring us to repentance.

The human heart may repeatedly resist the invitation of the Holy Spirit. God has granted us the freedom to reject Him as well as receive Him. He continues to pursue us with attempts to convince us of His love. Through the Holy Spirit, God attempts to bring us to an understanding of the truth. When we persist in our rebellion against God, we become calloused to the ministry of the Holy Spirit. We are less and less sensitive to the "still small voice" (1 Kings 19:12, KJV). Finally, we can become so hardened to spiritual things that we no longer sense the work of the Holy Spirit.

It is this condition that Jesus sees in the teachers of the Law. Or at the least He sees that they are in imminent danger of arriving at this spiritual state. If we have deadened our souls to the Holy Spirit's ministry as the means of coming to repentance, then we are beyond repentance. The teachers of the Law had lost (or were near to losing) the ability to recognize good or to care whether they were good. Jesus had not stopped speaking to them. They simply were no longer listening.

The unpardonable sin is the unrepented sin. The person who is sensitive enough to the Holy Spirit to experience regret and desires to turn away from sin will always find God responsive and forgiving. Only sin that is repented can be forgiven.

The woman described at the beginning of this chapter was not guilty of the unpardonable sin. Her repentance and anguish over her sin was evidence that the Holy Spirit was still able to reach her. I hope someone finally helped her to understand that.

It is a curious irony that the person who is concerned about committing the unpardonable sin is almost certainly not guilty of it. On the other hand, the one who has committed the unpardonable sin will be happily indifferent to it. He or she is no longer interested in the pardon God offers.

Let me add one note of caution. It is never our place to decide who has committed the unpardonable sin. We cannot discern the realities of the human heart. The forgiveness of the dying thief on the cross with Christ should make us cautious. This hardened criminal would seem to us to be a poor candidate for salvation, but Jesus knew better.

So, was the preacher at the opening of this chapter wrong about the unpardonable sin? Yes and no. He was wrong in his portrayal of God rejecting a repentant seeker. However, he was right in his message of urgency. He correctly reminded us that our decision in any moment of time may have ultimate consequences. Our eternal salvation may hinge on our response to the urging of the Holy Spirit at any point. The determining factor is not that God would cease to offer forgiveness. Rather it is that we would no longer have any interest in that forgiveness. God is persistent and long-suffering in His pursuit of us, but we should not forget that we will at some point make a final decision.

Only One Sin

The second lesson of Mark 3:28-29 is that there is only one unpardonable sin. Jesus tells us that all blasphemies except this one may be forgiven. If that is true, we should understand other references in Scripture to unforgivable sin—or God's abandonment—in terms of this unpardonable sin.

King Saul, for instance, stands as a tragic example in the Old Testament of one who was separated from God. 1 Sam. 16:14 tells us, "The Spirit of the LORD had departed from Saul." That declaration is difficult to understand unless we consider it in light of Jesus' words in Mark. In that case, the Samuel passage is telling us that Saul had so hardened his heart that he was no longer receptive to God's Spirit. It was not God's arbitrary or malicious abandonment of Saul that left him in the state of separation from God. It was, rather, Saul's determined disobedience that produced a heart beyond God's reach. The only unpardonable sin is sin harbored in a hardened, unrepentant heart.

All Other Sins

The third lesson is the good news that all other sins can be forgiven. If God's forgiveness is desired, He is willing to give it. 1 John 1:9 is a promise without a disclaimer: "If we confess our sins, he is faithful and just and will forgive us our sins." Period. The fact that we are concerned about our spiritual welfare is evidence that the Holy Spirit can still reach us. Any sin that is repented can be forgiven. That's good news!

Rachel shared her story with me. It was a sad, sordid

story of brokenness. She peeled back layers of shame to show me who she really was and what she had done. The question behind every disclosure was, "God couldn't love and forgive me for this, could He?" She was sure that she had gone too far and was beyond the reach of God's grace. Somewhere in that long litany of sin surely she had committed the "unpardonable" one. Not true. Forgiveness may be ours for the asking.

The good news for Rachel and for us is that God continues to offer His grace to us no matter what we have done. As long as the Holy Spirit is able to touch our hearts, bringing conviction that is met with repentance, we are not guilty of the unpardonable sin.

In his book *The Great Divorce,* C. S. Lewis offers a helpful insight. He concludes that, in the end, there will only be two kinds of people: those who finally allow God to do with them what *He* wills and those whom God finally allows to do with themselves what *they* will. Lewis reminds us that the ultimate decision rests with us. God has granted us that awesome power.

For those who seek Him, God extends open arms of forgiving and restoring grace. He is the waiting, loving Father in the parable of the prodigal son. The sinner who repents finds grace.

Others may choose not to seek Him. God is faithful in allowing us the freedom to exercise that choice. He will not override our will, forcing us to turn to Him. Persistent, determined resistance to His invitation will eventually harden our hearts. We will be desensitized to the ministry of the Holy Spirit. Finally, God will release us to have our own way.

Then, and only then, will we have committed the unpardonable sin.

*Name has been changed.

THE UESTION

*"How can prayer really change anything if You always
work according to Your will anyway?"*

THE | SSUES

- Why should I pray? Is it just wasted effort, or
  does God answer prayer?
- Does God care enough to listen to me?
- Does God ever change His mind?

BACKGROUND SCRIPTURE:

Exod. 32; Jon. 3 and 4; Matt. 26:36-46; Rom. 8:26-39

9

Does Prayer Really Change Anything?

by George Lyons

BEFORE I PRESUME to speak for God, I must acknowledge the obvious—I am not God.

But, then, neither are you.

Whatever we say about God depends primarily on what God has revealed in Scripture. We may also appeal to our own experience of God and to that of other believers across the centuries. Assuming that God is dependable and consistent with His revealed character, we can make some reasonable conclusions.[1] But we must never forget that, since we are not God, we will never understand all there is to know about Him. "God's . . . wisdom and knowledge have no end! No one can explain the things God decides or understand his ways" (Rom. 11:33, NCV).

Dr. George Lyons is a professor of religion at Northwest Nazarene College in Nampa, Idaho.

1. This is a self-conscious attempt to approach the solution by appeal to the so-called Wesleyan Quadrilateral. John Wesley identified the four sources of Christian theology as Scripture, tradition, reason, and experience. Scripture assumes the role of the norm, the primary source of authority in determining Christian truth.

Yet this awesome God invites us to pray. What an incredible privilege and responsibility! God desires our fellowship. He delights in our praise. But He also wants us to make our requests known (Phil. 4:6), to tell Him what we want. Scripture repeatedly affirms that God hears and answers our prayers.

Can Prayer Change God's Mind?

The questions remain:

- Do our prayers change God's mind?
- Or does prayer only change us so that we request what He has chosen to do on His own?
- Does God predetermine the future? Does He foreknow it?
- Must even God accept that what will be will be?
- Is He limited by past decisions that He and others have made, like it or not?
- Or is He willing and able to change?

A few Scripture passages seem to insist that God is not like human beings, who change their minds. At the very least such sections reveal that God does not lie. He keeps His promises. He is dependable. He is not fickle.

Dozens of other passages insist that God does change His mind. At the very least such texts reveal a God who is free to change His mind. Who is not trapped in His own universe. Who is creative and flexible enough to adjust to whatever humans may do to frustrate His plans.

In this light, the familiar passage, "Jesus Christ is the same yesterday and today and forever" (Heb. 13:8), cannot be taken as an affirmation of divine inflexibility, but as a statement of divine stability.

Let's weigh the biblical evidence. What, if anything, does prayer change?

Exhibit 1: The Golden Calf Incident

The golden calf incident, found in Exod. 32, presumes that God is free to change His mind, to modify His plans. It is the "stiff-necked" humans who seem resistant to change. Because of Israel's consistently rebellious ways, God revealed to Moses His intention to destroy them and begin a new nation with Moses as the founder. Moses could not deny the facts, but he could pray. And he did. In response to Moses' prayer, "The LORD relented and did not bring on his people the disaster he had threatened" (Exod. 32:14).

The Hebrew word translated "relented" in the *New International Version* is translated "repented" in both the King James and *Revised Standard Version*. Both the *New Century Version* and the *New Revised Standard Version* say "the LORD changed his mind" about His plans.

We must not misunderstand divine repentance. The Hebrew word translated "repent" in the Old Testament as applied to God's activity does not mean a turning from sin. It refers instead to His reluctance to follow through on His threats of judgment. It highlights His change of attitude and behavior. Not only is God is free in theory to change His plans, but He actually does so.

Still, God is not fickle. He is definitely dependable. Because He keeps His promises, He can always be counted on to act in ways that are consistently gracious and redemptive.

God "repents" in response to the prayers of the righteous in behalf of unrepentant sinners. God's threatened judgment on Israel is softened by Moses' intercession. God's repentance reveals His character: "The LORD, the LORD, the compassionate and gracious God, slow to anger, abounding in love and faithfulness, maintaining love to thousands, and forgiving wickedness, rebellion and sin" (Exod. 34:6-7).

Exhibit 2: The Case of the Reluctant Prophet

The Book of Jonah contains only one prophecy: "After forty days, Nineveh will be destroyed!" (Jon. 3:4, NCV). There is no explicit condition attached, such as: "unless the people of Nineveh repent of their sins." However, because they do repent and because God is faithful to His character of redemptive love, God repents. He relents and changes His mind. Nineveh is spared—to Jonah's dismay. The reluctant prophet is scandalized by this "gracious and compassionate God, slow to anger and abounding in love, a God who relents from sending calamity" (4:2).

This is no exception; it is the biblical norm. God consistently changes His mind about threatened judgment in response to people who repent of their sinful ways. But if God's people turn from obedience to rebellion, God is also free to change His mind about the blessings of salvation He has promised them. Despite His gracious deliverance of Israel from Egyptian bondage. Despite the miraculous victory at the Red Sea. Even despite the covenant established at Mount Sinai, Exod. 32 reveals that God was fully prepared to destroy His unfaithful people. He is a God of uncompromising holiness, but His mercy overpowers His justice in response to Moses' prayer.

Implication 1: Prayer Changes God's Mind

All this suggests that God acts in response to prayer in ways He would not otherwise. If God is genuinely free to change His mind in response to our prayers, the implications are mind-boggling. If God has granted us the freedom to persist in rebellion or to repent of our sins, many popular notions about God are in need of revision. If changing one's mind is actually possible—whether God's mind or ours—then the future is not an already finished script written in timeless eternity and only played out in time.

If God does graciously change His mind in response to humans, which future did He foreknow? A future with Nineveh destroyed or spared? A future with Israelites or "Mosesites"? Were God's threats of judgment empty promises, or was He genuinely prepared to do what He said? What if Jonah had not preached in Nineveh, however reluctantly? What if the Ninevites had not repented? What if Israel had not made the golden calf? What if Moses had not interceded when he did? Did Moses' prayers genuinely change the mind of God? Does human perversity or human prayer actually reshape the course of history? Unless God only pretends to change His mind, unless prayers of repentance and intercession are only superficial exercises, then the future cannot be described as etched in stone.

This is not to deny God's omniscience. It only discredits popular notions of what knowing everything must involve. God knows all that is knowable. What God chooses not to know is not knowable, because the all-knowing, all-powerful God has chosen to grant human beings the freedom to choose right or wrong.

This does not deny God's omnipotence. God could create a rock so big He couldn't move it. He chooses not to because the task is ridiculous, not because His power is limited. It is equally foolish to expect God to know fully a future that depends, in part, on the free decisions of others and on His own freedom to change His mind. The future is open to change, because an almighty, holy, infinitely patient God chooses to be redemptive. He chooses to allow us to participate in His redemptive purposes through our prayers and obedience.

Because God is omnipotent, He can do all that He chooses to do. Because He is omniscient, He knows all that He chooses to know. Because God is eternal, He can wait as long as it takes to accomplish His purposes. Because

God is redemptive, He is absolutely free to be responsive to His creation. He is free to change His mind without being fickle.

The future is not written in granite. Apparently, names can be both added to and blotted from the Book of Life (see Exod. 32:32; Rev. 3:5; 22:19). People once "saved" can be lost, and those once "lost" can be saved (see Ezek. 18). We are not simply playing out some eternally prescribed and divinely foreknown script. Because God has determined that His ultimate purposes for this world will be achieved by persuasion—or coercion if necessary—predictive prophecy is possible. But most prophecies about the future come with an explicit or implicit attachment—"unless."

God has chosen to act in ways that are consistently responsive to what His creatures choose to do. Since He knows us fully and intimately, He knows everything we are capable of doing. He is never taken by surprise. Because He is faithful to His revealed character, because He keeps His promises, even God is, to a certain extent, predictable. God can be trusted to keep faith with fickle people and yet fulfill His promises.[2]

Implication 2: Prayer Changes Us

Let us be careful not to go from one mistaken extreme to another. We do not pray because God needs our advice as to how to run the universe. God is not sitting on His throne waiting for our prayers so He can decide what to do next. We do not need to pray because God is indecisive or uncertain as to what is best. We do not pray because God is lonely and needs our company. God the Father lived through countless ages of eternity with only the company

---

2. At several points in the above discussion I refer to the fuller treatment of this subject found in my article "The God Who Changes His Mind," in *The Preacher's Magazine* (March—May 1993): 30-33.

of the Son and Holy Spirit before He began the project we call creation.

We pray because we need God's fellowship. We pray because we need to learn what He wants for and from us—and His creation. With Jesus we sometimes struggle to come to the point in our prayers when we can say and mean, "Not what I want, but what you want" (Mark 14:36, NRSV). Indeed, while we believe "prayer changes things," more importantly prayer changes *us*.

Exhibit 3: The Example of Jesus

Heb. 5:7 records this observation: "During the days of Jesus' life on earth, he offered up prayers and petitions with loud cries and tears to the one who could save him from death, and he was heard because of his reverent submission." This clearly alludes to Jesus' agonizing struggle in the Garden of Gethsemane.

The burden of Jesus' repeated prayer was for His Father to spare Him the experience of the "cup." Whatever the dregs of this cup may have involved—suffering, death, separation from friends, separation from His Father, bearing the sins of the world—most of us would read this story as one of unanswered prayer. What Jesus requested, His Father denied.

Hebrews puts the story in an entirely different light. It insists that Jesus "was heard." The clear implication of this is that the Father answered His prayer. As 1 John 5:15 puts it, "And if we know that [God] hears us—whatever we ask—we know that we have what we asked of him."

As we know, Jesus died. Yes, God raised Him from the dead. Perhaps, this is what the author had in mind when he wrote Jesus "was heard because of his reverent submission" (Heb. 5:7). Three days is not a long wait for an answer to prayer under most circumstances. Awaiting an answer to prayer in the face of death is an entirely different matter. Despite His death, God answered His prayer for deliverance by means of the Resurrection. We believe that, despite the certainty of our deaths, perfect healing awaits us in the resurrection.

It was Jesus' prayer that God's will should be done, despite His personal preferences, that was answered. The death of Jesus Christ was the necessary condition for our salvation. We thank God that Jesus was not granted His preferred answer, that the "cup" be avoided.

So, what if God answers our prayers in the same way? What if we never see the answers until after our deaths? So what?

Rom. 8:28 has been a comfort to many believers across the centuries, but too many of us ignore its biblical context. Verse 29 makes it clear that God's intention for all believers is that we should be conformed to the likeness of Jesus Christ.

We sing, "O to be like Thee, blessed Redeemer—this is my constant longing and prayer." But do we mean it? We want to be more loving and kind. We want to be more patient and holy. But do we really want to be like Jesus? The path to Christlikeness includes suffering and, at the end, a cross. It includes "prayers and petitions with loud cries and tears." It includes apparently "unanswered" prayers. Can we trust that God hears even the prayer that seems to go unanswered?

Implication 3: Prayer Changes the World

Our assignment on this planet is not to identify specific answers to specific prayers. It is to be submissive to God. If we are, we can be sure, God will hear our prayers. Let us learn to leave the answers and the timing to Him. Just think of the mess we'd be in if God had answered Jesus' prayer in the Garden as He asked!

The disciples' prayer—"Your kingdom come, your

will be done on earth as it is in heaven" (Matt. 6:10)—is not a prayer of *resignation*. It is not simply accepting the inevitable: "Well, God, You're going to do what You want anyway, regardless of what I want. So help me to accept it. Help me to learn to like it." Not at all.

This is a prayer of *realignment*. We pray in this way so that we may enter into a relationship with God that enables us to know Him better. In prayer we learn what God loves. We learn what breaks His heart. We learn what gives Him joy. We come to share His dreams and aspirations for us and the world. We are grasped by His love that will not let us go. Love that desires what is in our eternal best interests. Love that longs to make us all we can be by His grace.

This is a prayer of *realization*. Because we learn "what God's will is—his good, pleasing and perfect will" (Rom. 12:2), we long to see His kingdom come. We long to see rebellion quelled and the rightful Ruler of the universe recognized. We commit ourselves to participating in His redemptive purposes. To undoing the havoc sinful humans have wreaked on this planet. To restoring humankind to the freedom we surrendered when we threw off divine constraint and insisted on having our own way. We pray because alone we cannot accomplish what we want, much less what He wants. The problems in our world are insurmountable in human strength alone. So we pray—and obey.

THE  UESTION

"There is so much violence and lawlessness around us. What are You doing about it, and why do You let it continue?"

THE | SSUES

- Why doesn't an all-powerful God protect us from violence?
- Is violence getting progressively worse?
- Who is winning—God and His kingdom of peace or the anarchy of sin, selfishness, and violence?

BACKGROUND SCRIPTURE:

Exod. 20:13; Ps. 68:5-6; Isa. 9:6-7;
Matt. 5:9, 38-39; Luke 2:13-14; Heb. 10:23

10

Will Somebody Please Stop the Violence?

by Rebecca Laird

D URING ADVENT one year, the Scriptures we read on Sunday seemed incongruous to the nightly news. In church we read, "For to us a child is born . . . And he will be called Wonderful Counselor, Mighty God, Everlasting Father, Prince of Peace. Of the increase of his government and peace there will be no end" (Isa. 9:6-7).

Within a week, a man consumed by racial rage shot and killed six commuters returning from New York City. I live close to where this tragedy occurred and regularly travel to the city by train. I could have easily been one of his victims. Where was the Prince of Peace and His peaceful government? It seemed rather that "of violence there will be no end."

The next week my family traveled to Denver to visit relatives. The day we arrived, a disgruntled ex-employee

---

Rebecca Laird is a writer and editor specializing in adult spirituality and social renewal. She is co-author of *No Hiding Place: Recovery and Empowerment for Our Troubled Communities.* She is a member of the Lamb's Church of the Nazarene, Manhattan, New York.

at a pizza parlor murdered his former boss. A few days later the media reported a threat from a disturbed soul who vowed to shoot Santa in a mall. The area shopping centers closed "Santa Lands." We parents tried to answer our bewildered children's question, "Why does somebody want to kill Santa Claus?"

On Sunday we sang, "Hark! the herald angels sing ' . . . Peace on earth, and mercy mild—God and sinners reconciled.'" Where was that reconciliation?

With all this lawlessness and violence not far from my mind, my family joined the worldwide Christian church in retelling the glorious story: "Suddenly a great company of the heavenly host appeared with the angel, praising God and saying, 'Glory to God in the highest, and on earth peace to men on whom his favor rests'" (Luke 2:13-14).

In a stable, God humbly entered into the human struggle as a helpless baby. The Child grew and took upon His shoulders the sins (violence and brokenness) of His brothers and sisters of the world. As an adult, Jesus called many to join Him in living a new way.

That Christmas, I wondered anew about the teachings of Jesus. Especially His proclamation, "Blessed are the peacemakers, for they will be called [children] of God" (Matt. 5:9). Peacemakers are few and far between. Violence rages. What does it mean for us to be people of peace in a society where those who love guns and hate others (and probably themselves) hold us hostage to fear?

The Problem of Violence

Violence isn't a new phenomenon. Assuming that ancient times were more peaceful is wishful thinking. Jesus was born into Palestine where Roman rule was heavy and oppression was real. Cross the Romans, and one would end up on a cross. Thousands were crucified for rebelling. Almost everybody was hoping for a messiah to come and end the political tyranny. Then Jesus arrived—teaching nonviolence, noncooperation with evil, and love for one's enemies!

Jesus did not appear as a conquering, political king. He came as a suffering servant who called those who would follow to love enemies—even oppressors!—with a deep love that supersedes unjust treatment. Jesus commanded that we respond with love—even risk receiving further damage—rather than take revenge or handle the offender as we have been wrongly treated.

Why did Jesus do this? Because to Jesus those who kill and maim are not enemies deserving retaliation. They are in need of forgiveness. As He said on the way to the Cross, "Father, forgive them, for they do not know what they are doing" (Luke 23:34).

Immediately after Jesus told us that peacemakers are blessed, He went on to preach in the Sermon on the Mount: "You have heard that it was said, 'Eye for eye, and tooth for tooth.' But I tell you, Do not resist an evil person. If someone strikes you on the right cheek, turn to him the other also" (Matt. 5:38-39).

I hear this verse and think, *Perhaps I would let someone strike me for the sake of love.* But today, fighting isn't done with hands—it's done with pistols, semiautomatic weapons, missiles, and nuclear warheads. If we let someone shoot once, there will be no need to turn the other cheek. We'll already be dead.

So what about Jesus' teaching? What does Matt. 5:38-39 mean? Ron Sider, in *Christ and Violence*, offers two insights. First, it means "that one should not resist evil persons by exacting equal damages for injury suffered." Second, it means "that one should not respond to an evil person by placing him in the category of enemy. Indeed, one should love one's enemies, even at great personal cost.

The good of the other person, not one's own needs or rights are decisive."[1]

Let me illustrate. A tormented young man in our community shot and killed a wonderful church woman. She was a saint and certainly didn't deserve it. She deserved a long life and lots of love. He, too, had gone to church, but sporadically. By murdering this woman, he became an enemy—someone to be feared and avoided.

What was the church to do? Buy guns and patrol the community to protect the single women? Never reach out to another tormented young man? And what about the murderer, a person for whom Christ died? We must (but who will?) continue to pray, visit, and love the unlovable. What hard words these are to live!

Does this mean that we must take every wrong done to us without a word? Or sit idly by as kids carry guns and kill each other for fun or out of frustration?

No. No. Absolutely, no!

Jesus compels us to be peacemakers, but not to lie down in the face of evil. We are to be clear and active in our noncooperation with evil. Jesus lived, and ultimately died, amid violence, all the while proclaiming and embodying the values of the kingdom of God. Jesus taught and lived forgiveness, holy power, and sacrificial love.

We are also required to be involved in peacemaking in our own cities and towns. We can't proclaim peace from the pulpits and pews without doing what we can to preserve the sacredness of human life in our homes, on our streets, and in our neighborhoods.

When we consider the mortal violence all around us, Jesus' call to respond to lawlessness with tough (i.e., non-sentimental) love challenges our commitments and models of ministry. We aren't called necessarily to wrestle guns out of the hands of thugs. Jesus isn't asking for martyrs but for followers who will act truthfully and let the outcome be left in God's hands—even at the risk of martyrdom. Remember, survival and safety are not gospel promises. Look at Jesus and His disciples—only a few lived to a ripe, old age.

Lethal violence demands a savvy response. When one person kills another, the one with the gun treats the other person as a thing. Christians cannot do that. People—all people—are created in the image of God. We can't shoot back; but we can fight back with love, courage, and shrewdness while balancing the issues of justice and mercy.

Violence and Values

How then do we deter violence? The key to reducing violence is found in imparting Kingdom values. What makes people kill and maim others?

Recently, a reporter for *Time* magazine asked some teenagers in a Midwestern city why they bought, carried, and used guns. One said, "It was always really violent around my house." One reason people resort to violence is they see others act in violent ways. Violence breeds violence. When kids watch parents, older siblings, and television heroes use force to get what they want, they emulate what they see.

The magazine reporter also said that kids used guns as "a defense against the inexplicable despair that torments so many . . . teenagers." Despair is living without hope. Many kids today spend their tender years with absent or too-busy parents. The voices that many hear for hours each day are those of older kids in the neighborhood who have discovered that guns bring a sense of power. In overly simplistic terms, some embrace the values of violence that say, "So what if we never have a stable family? So what if we don't go to school and can't get a job? There aren't any jobs anyway! Nobody cares about me, why should I care about anyone or anything else? Why not get a gun and use it? I probably won't live to adulthood anyway. If people won't respect me, at least they will fear me."

Lastly, the reporter wrote that, "Some days, guns are just a defense against boredom that comes from a lack of guidance and direction."[2] Many kids are left to their own devices, and guns are at least one form of excitement. Having a group of kids that will take one's side no matter what happens is almost as good as having a loving family. Most will take belonging to a gang over going it alone. That's very human of them.

The Church as an Agent of Peace

Violence is rooted in misplaced values. People kill because they don't understand that life is a sacred gift from God. Ironic, isn't it, that one of the clearest commandments we have is "You shall not murder" (Exod. 20:13)? How come these kids never learned this? If parents and schools failed to teach basic values, where was the church?

People also resort to violence because they feel powerless, unloved, and outcast. Our Bible proclaims, "A father of the fatherless and a judge for widows, is God in His holy habitation. God makes a home for the lonely" (Ps. 68:5-6, NASB). Are we emulating our God? Are we mentoring the kids without parents? Are we defending and including the vulnerable in our communities?

People resort to violence because they have no hope. Certainly one of the things the church has in quantity is hope. Heb. 10:23-24 says, "Let us hold unswervingly to the hope we profess, for he who promised is faithful. And let us consider how we may spur one another on toward love and good deeds." What are we doing to encourage one another to declare peace and show love in the world and in our neighborhoods?

Christians are called not to violence, but to value the sanctity of life. We preach that all are welcome in the family of God and that hope is available through faith. The church has something vital to offer as an alternative to violence.

Just as the Christmas of violence I described above erupted, nearly 50 religious leaders from across the country praised the president of the United States for his declaration of values as central to curbing violence. The letter they sent to the White House said, "The battle against violence begins in each of our hearts and lives. Religious faith offers vital moral resources for replacing fear and violence with hope and reconciliation in our homes, communities, and nation."[3]

Here are a few examples of what various churches are doing to instill values that promote peace and deter violence.

Prevention programs: The best time to deter violence is before it begins.

A minister in central New Jersey says, "There aren't many institutions set up to win people over to a value system. It's up to the church to show that a prescribed set of values is possible."[4] One of the concrete things his church does is to have all of the children bring in their report cards, which are entered into a data base. Any child that gets under a "B" is given a tutor. Additionally, boys from single-parent families are paired with men as role models.

A church in San Francisco opened its doors and invited the addicts in the neighborhood to come in and talk about why they smoked crack cocaine. Drug addiction and violence go hand in glove. Many crimes are committed to obtain money for drugs, and many violent acts are committed by persons under the influence of drugs and alcohol. The addicts talked about smoking crack to deaden the pain of family abuse, shame, and deprivation. As relationships began and the church became an extended family for the addicts, a grassroots recovery program was designed by the recovering addicts and spread out into the community. Violent crime decreased in their neighborhood.

Another church in California hosted a course for parents of children at risk in the local elementary school. Parents were recruited through personal calls and mailings by the program director. The church provided the facility, baby-sitters, tutors, and follow-up. Parishioners came and cheered on the graduates who completed the 12-week course on positive parenting skills.

Outreach programs: Many persons don't belong to a local congregation. Thus, the church must stay in or go to troubled neighborhoods and offer hope and help.

Groups of people from various churches rallied in Maryland to support handgun legislation and stood vigil on corners frequented by drug dealers. Nothing is so successful in deterring drugs and crime as good people banding together with their eyes wide open.

In Oakland, California, a congregation in an inner-city neighborhood facilitated dialogue sessions between gang members and local police. Church members, along with representatives from other denominations, held weekly prayer vigils at the site of the numerous homicides committed earlier in the year. The church also responded to a request to help stop vandalism by sponsoring block parties in the neighborhoods where vandalism and violence reigned. People got to know each other and began working together. Vandalism fell drastically.

It is well-known that crime soars in the summer months when kids are bored and unsupervised. In the northeast, a group of college students designed a program for the teens in a high-crime housing project during after-school and summer hours. The students staffed a community center that offers an alternative to violence. Many kids chose basketball games and trips to the beach over driving around town aimlessly with loaded guns ready to use on a whim. As one youth worker in the Bronx said, "Kids aren't stupid. If you offer them a clean glass of water or a dirty glass of water, they'll take the clean one." Sadly, too few glasses of clean water are being offered.

Many churches have taken on violence by committing to prison ministries. People coming out of prison are at risk to commit further crimes as many remain without jobs, support, or motivation to reenter society. The families of the incarcerated also are at high risk of continuing the cycle of violence and criminal behavior without the intervention of others who model a different way of living.

Political action: In San Francisco, a local church invited the precinct police to come to the church and teach the congregation how to protect themselves and deter others from violence. A community watch was organized, and neighbors began to patrol their neighborhoods and assist those in need. The church gained the respect of its neighbors and several started coming to church as a result. They realized that the church cared about the community.

In New York state, clergy launched a campaign against handguns and semiautomatic weapons and met with media executives to complain about violence in programming and reporting on news shows. To complement this program, clergy vowed to encourage boycotts of advertisers that sponsored violent programming.

In Petaluma, California, local churches rallied and petitioned lawmakers to pass a "three-strikes-you're-out" law that would mandate life sentences for repeat felons.

The church has power to pass on values, advocate for good, and resist evil and violence. Promoting peace will challenge us deeply.

So, Who's Winning?

With the increasing volume of violence all around us, we may be tempted to ask ourselves (in a voice hopefully loud enough for God to eavesdrop), "Who's winning?" Goodness, peace, and love? Or sin, hate, and violence? The newspapers seem to report the score in favor of the latter. But the view from the newspapers doesn't cover the whole story.

As Christians we have the assurance that, while violence may appear to have the upper hand, there is more to life than can be seen. The steadily growing, relentless kingdom of God moves ahead in ways sometimes too subtle for human perception. That's the way the Kingdom has impacted our violent world from the day an innocent baby was born in a manger while would-be assassins lurked in the shadows. God's kingdom is winning and will ultimately disarm those whose aim is destruction and violence. It is this indisputable hope that carries those who day after day offer peace and love to their troubled world.

The story is told that after the crumbling of the Iron Curtain and the abrupt end of decades of communistic rule in one of the eastern European countries, a Protestant church reopened. The church board met to decide what message should be put on their outside sign to alert the town that the church was again in operation, having survived the violent and atheistic leadership imposed on them.

After prayerful and careful consideration, the board posted this simple message, "The Lamb wins!" In spite of the power of the seemingly invincible communist state, in the end the Kingdom was declared the winner. And not just at the end, but to unseeing eyes the Kingdom was winning all along.

The Lamb wins! In the face of violence, injustice, corruption, and sin, God is working His purposes out through those of us who claim the name of Christ. We know that the Prince of Peace has come, and we, as His followers, have been empowered to do all we can to bring peace to our tumultuous society.

NOTES

1. Ron Sider, *Christ and Violence* (Scottdale, Pa.: Herald Press, 1979), 47.

2. Jon D. Hull, "A Boy and His Gun," *Time* 142, 5 (August 2, 1993), 21-27.

3. "Believers Strive to Stem Violence," *The Christian Century* (January 26, 1994), 69.

4. Ruth Bonapace, "Churches as the 'Only Hope' for Change," *The New York Times* (February 6, 1994), 3.

THE **Q**UESTION

"Everyone says You have a 'plan for my life.'
How do I find out what that plan is?"

THE **I**SSUES

- Why is it so hard to find God's plan?
- What happens if I make a mistake about God's plan for my life?
- If God makes His plan so hard to discover, what happens if I ignore His plan?

BACKGROUND SCRIPTURE:

Exod. 19:5-6*a*; Pss. 100:3; 119:9-16; John 3:16-18; Gal. 5:16-17, 24-25; Eph. 4:1-7, 11-24; Col. 3:17; 1 Thess. 5:23-24; 1 Pet. 2:9; Rev. 1:5*b*-6

11

God Has a Wonderful Plan for Your Life

by Randall Davey

A SATURDAY NIGHT Youth for Christ rally in Canton, Ohio, was the place. "God has a wonderful plan for your life" was the gist of the message. I was a 13-year-old kid. I was one of the few teens in the Cambridge, Ohio, church when my pastor, Rev. Jim Fox, took a liking to me and hauled me some 60 miles in his aging Pontiac to watch a Christian magician "magish."

The magician was a warmhearted, friendly sort and appeared to be harmless. He did one trick after another and talked without benefit of breathing. Somewhere between pulling a rabbit out of a hymnal and making a parrot quote Ps. 119:11, he pulled a minisermon out of his hat and most of us were none the wiser. I don't have a clue as to the text, but I remember the main point. He said it a zillion times. "God has a wonderful plan for your life."

With near-lightning speed, he was back to rabbits and

Randall Davey is senior pastor of the Church of the Nazarene, Fairfield Village, Pennsylvania.

doves, and then gave a pitch for missionaries to Africa. "How many of you are willing to go to the mission field if that is God's plan for your life?" I was lost. I thought it must be some trick, figuring that if I raised my hand in answer to his question, he would make an eagle rest on my thumb. I didn't move a limb, but kids all around me did. Minutes after the service ended, I walked through a crowd of Albert Schweitzer wanna-bes and sidled up to the magician. I asked him to sign a program for my "little" brother, betting that he wouldn't know my brother was eight years my senior and was actually doing a military stint in Germany.

On the trip home, Rev. Fox started the interrogation. "What did you think of the magician?" "Did you like the evening?" "Would you like to come back?" "What do you think God's plan is for your life?"

I was speechless. Not too many years earlier, I was convinced that my fate would be riding the range, killing off evil types lingering close to the OK Corral. I didn't figure God into that equation.

God's Wonderful Plan for My Life

I wasn't able to shake the question about God's plan. It was never far from my mind. The Africa thing plagued me. I'm not into snakes, never liked major heat, and didn't feel especially good about loincloths. Surely God wouldn't want me to go to the mission field. The more I thought about it, the more I didn't want to think about it.

In time, with fewer trips to Canton, I was able to shake the Africa idea. But the older I got, a new question seemed to be equally pressing and dangerously similar. It was the "God's will" question.

For reasons I'll never understand, I locked on to the idea that both God's plan and God's will were fairly limited to a particular job. The "God's plan" question was really just a spiritually upscale version of, "What do you want to be when you get big?" The new twist was that God was deciding, not me.

College promised to be a time of delay. I wouldn't have to declare God's plan for a few years, so I thought I could put the question on hold. But when I couldn't choose between a holiness college in California and the new one in nearby Mount Vernon, Ohio, my pastor encouraged me to seek God's will as to which school I should attend. That process didn't take too long. My folks said that if I wanted to go to Mount Vernon, they would help finance my education; but if I chose California, I would go it alone. My heart felt "strangely warmed" to stay in Ohio, and I was soon to testify that it was God's will that I be part of the pioneer class at Mount Vernon.

In the early days at college, I was overwhelmed with the frequency with which "God's will" came into everyday conversation. Folks were quitting school, getting engaged, or joining the foreign legion—all in the name of "God's will." A professor took it one step further, saying that God told him which car to buy and when to leave one job to take another. By the end of one semester, I had reached the firm conclusion that God was a whole lot more talkative with some folks than He seemed to be with me.

I did two years of college in Ohio and two years in Massachusetts. Chapel messages during those days blend together in my memory. But more than once, I heard reference to God's "best." Poor choices along the way could force one into God's "second best," and it seemed to go downhill from there. Stories of should-have-been-missionaries who were now bitter hardware clerks linger in my mind. Clearly, I didn't want God's "second" or "third" best. And I had no desire to clerk in a hardware store.

Still, in honest pursuit of God's plan and God's will, I picked up on the "open-door" philosophy. While praying at an altar in the barn-turned-chapel, a sincere counselor explained, "If you don't know God's will, tell Him that you're open to it. And if it's still not clear, tell Him you plan to go through door A. And unless God closes the door, you can assume it is His will." As much as I appreciated the counsel, it sounded too much like "Let's Make a Deal."

I graduated from college and went to seminary for one, express purpose—I wanted to know more of the God who makes plans and has a will and keeps them both a secret from guys like me. I wasn't at all convinced that I would ever take a degree from the seminary or do something so "unthinkable" as pastor a church. I just wanted to take a year to focus on knowing God and to address the torment I felt over not knowing His perfect will and wonderful plan.

Well, I stayed, graduated, and have pastored since 1975. During those years, I have reached some working conclusions. As the late Bertha Munro, former dean of my alma mater, was prone to say, "The years teach."

The Years Teach

I'm not inclined to argue with persons who say, "God has a wonderful plan for your life, and it is His will that we do it." I am far more likely to talk about it differently— cautiously and reverently. I'm increasingly sensitive to folk who use "God's will" as an explanation for decisions on which they don't want to be challenged. I'm thinking of a church staff person who resigned from his post offering no explanation. He left the church he served in a lurch, confused, and hurt while he glibly offered the line, "I've prayed about it, and I know it's God's will." Why would God do such a thing? And the story didn't have a happy-ever-after conclusion. I think that borders on taking the Lord's name in vain.

These days, I'm far more inclined to talk about God's

overarching plan for humankind and find it to be a good starting point for more specific concerns. Until these foundational plans are understood, I'm not sure more focused plans make sense.

Foundational Plans

God's wonderful plan includes saving His people. Since Red Sea days, God has been acting throughout history in saving ways. The apex of His saving work was seen in the life, death, and resurrection of Jesus Christ who died for the whole world (see John 3:16). As clearly, it is His will to set His people apart for His agenda. In other words, it is His will to sanctify His people (see 1 Thess. 5:23).

God's wonderful plan includes raising up a radically different community of people who will boldly confess the risen Lord in worship and in life. While the world rushes head-long to worship athletes and acquisitions, God plans for the Body of Christ (i.e., the Church) to model an alternative way of living that is inclusive—crossing racial, ethnic, economic, gender, and age barriers. That alternative way of living is best expressed when persons of every age, color and race gather in one place at one time to confess that Jesus Christ is Lord.

This community will be marked by persons who have hidden God's Word in their hearts (see Ps. 119:11) while doing what they do in the name of the Lord (see Col. 3:17).

God's wonderful plan includes giving His people a God-birthed identity. Collectively, believers are the "priesthood of believers." Individually, then, they are "priests" as seen in both the Old and New Testaments. Exod. 19:6 references a "kingdom of priests." So does 1 Pet. 2:9, "You are a chosen people, a royal priesthood." Likewise, Rev. 1:6 says, "And [Jesus] has made us to be a kingdom [of] priests."

God's wonderful plan includes using His people as

priests to reach unsaved people. God plans to use everyone He saves to participate in the saving action of others. Perhaps comparable to Isaiah, who, in the face of the holy "Other," confessed, found forgiveness, and then offered himself in service. (See Isa. 6:1-8.) How can we do any less?

Before assuming that this has vocational implications, consider this: The Bible seems to teach that all who believe are made new creatures in Christ and are given not only an *identity* (that of priest) but a *function* as well. Believers are given the ministry of reconciliation, both to become reconciled to God ourselves and to bring fellow human beings to God (see 2 Cor. 5:17-20).

It follows, then, that saved persons of every kind are given the central privilege of participating in the ministry of reconciliation. That is not tied to vocation. Converted tentmakers or business owners, affluent or homeless, all are given the same ministry.

God's wonderful plan includes training His reconciliation-driven priests for service. That's the business of pastors. After leading believers in worship, the primary task of clergy is to train believers for the ministry of priesthood and the work of reconciliation (see Eph. 4:11-13).

God's wonderful plan also includes giving the spirit in which all that is done in Christ's name is to be done. That's important to understand. One can be quite clear on identity and function but out of line in terms of spirit.

A few years ago, I was in the hospital for several days and met nurses of every stripe. The head nurse in particular fascinated me. I watched her dutifully come into my room, check the IV, take vital signs, and—just as dutifully—leave. She only spoke when spoken to, and even then, the response was clipped and formal. I didn't doubt her competency for a moment, but I really took issue with her spirit that I deemed far more suitable in a veterinary clinic than a hospital.

What is the spirit in which Christ's people do "God's wonderful plan"? I would think "[with] grace and truth" (John 1:14) might be an appropriate answer.

I've seen more than a few servants of God preach, teach the Word, or go door to door visiting. Yet, the spirit in which some of them did the good deed was less than infectious, if not outright condemning. Surely God's plan includes a people known for being a people of grace.

God's wonderful plan includes those who are tapped for particular service in the Body of Christ. Pastors, teachers, missionaries, counselors, and caregivers, as well as other servants of various kinds, are persons who frequently give witness to a compelling call to serve God in a unique way, at a particular place, and for a given time. They serve shoulder to shoulder with scores of folk not so easily identified as "ministers," but who are equally valuable in the Body of Christ.

So What About His Specific Plan for Me?

I believe that God calls and equips some persons to serve His Church in unique ways. I believe beyond question that He moves certain individuals to serve in far-off places. But I am equally convinced that He more broadly calls all who take on the name of Christ to be people of the "plan." Disciples, if you will, who move through life taking moment-by-moment cues from Him, in keeping with the spirit and intent of His revealed and inspired Word. More simply put, we are to be "imitators . . . of the Lord" (1 Thess. 1:6), bent on His agenda.

Only after we have discovered and followed God's larger agenda can we address the issue of how to face specific decisions that come our way. How do we know if a particular action is part of God's broad plan for our lives? Honest answers to several questions can help us know.

1. **Search the Scriptures.** Does the Bible give clear in-

struction about the matter? Or does the Bible specifically forbid such action?

2. **Is it right?** Does the action we are contemplating violate any moral or ethical norms? Does the step we are considering lead toward personal spiritual growth? Will it help us to "continue to work out [our] salvation"? (Phil. 2:12).

3. **Is it providential?** Can we clearly see how God is at work in the situation? Can we feel the prompting of the Holy Spirit telling us to do this?

4. **Is it reasonable?** Does it help to build stronger connections in the community of faith? Or is it so extreme as to be divisive and hurtful? Does it fit into the pattern that God already is developing in our lives?

After such careful consideration, we will know we are living out our lives as people of the "plan." We will be better able to confess the Lord in worship and life. It will facilitate us reaching the unsaved with the message of reconciliation. A spirit of "grace and truth" will increase.

Frankly, I grieve for the many who were sold on the idea that God ordained them, for example, a businessperson and then left them alone to make a fortune. We are called to follow Jesus *daily* (Luke 9:23). God saves for a purpose. He sanctifies for a reason. We are His possessions. "Know that the LORD is God. It is he who made us, and we are his; we are his people, the sheep of his pasture" (Ps. 100:3).

Does God Have a Wonderful Plan for My Life?

Surely, the answer is yes. He does. The plan is both broad and narrow, general and specific, obvious and subtle. It's His way, not our way.

We will surely find His will if we live by the Spirit, walk by the Spirit, and live in peace (see Gal. 5).

THE **Q**UESTION

*"At the age of 75 years,
how do I best serve God and my family?"*

THE **I**SSUES

- Is "old" the same as "bad"?
- I feel left out as an older person even though I have a lot to give.
- What does God think about old persons?

BACKGROUND SCRIPTURE:

Ps. 71:17-18; Phil. 3:12-14; 2 Tim. 4:7-8

12

Never Too Old

by Vicki Hesterman

SOMEHOW, I NEVER THOUGHT of Gram as retired. She just kept baking bread for her family and friends, writing encouraging letters, praying for us all. Feisty and funny, she was a woman of God, and I always knew it.

Helen Ide, my high school home economics teacher and our pastor's wife, didn't really retire either, although she finished her public school teaching career. Widowed and living far from her family, she started a ministry in her little town, teaching underprivileged women mothering skills.

Sunday School teacher Mrs. Brier always had a sweet smile and a friendly word. When she was confined to her bed with illness a few years before she died, she became a prayer warrior. Her unwavering faith inspired all of us who knew her. She was also a great encouragement to our young pastor and his wife.

My parents have always given generously of their time and resources to our little church. Now that they are retired from their professions, they continue to care about their church and community. My grandparents, too, were

---

Dr. Vicki Hesterman is a professor of journalism at Point Loma Nazarene College, San Diego.

beautiful examples of Christians who kept the faith through both triumphs and tragedies.

My surviving grandmother continues to quietly affirm God's faithfulness as she visits frail patients in nursing homes, keeps in touch with family members, and participates in church mission groups. At 85, she has been widowed twice and survived a serious heart attack, but she concentrates on what she still can do. I treasure the little notes of encouragement she sends from time to time.

I think of so many others who inspire me. They just keep right on helping in whatever ways they can. I well remember my Sunday School and Bible study teachers in a tiny Ohio town. To this day, when I visit my parents' church, these beautiful folks stop to say hello. They walk more slowly down that church aisle now—some use canes and walkers—but they still worship, they still encourage others, and they still pray. Even those who are gone left a legacy of love and concern—in the books and tapes they donated to the library, in the children and teens they taught about God's Word, and in the love and encouragement they gave so freely.

Changing Demographics

Who are these "older folks" who have moved into their 50s, 60s, and 70s? They are a large and significant segment of our population.

The statistics are amazing. Today the United States has more persons 65 years of age and older than the entire population of Canada (26,000,000). The fastest growing group of people is over 55—growing three times faster than the population at large. Since 1982, we have more persons over 65 than under 18. Scientists predict life expectancy will increase from 75 years to 80 years within the decade.

Our society is rapidly moving from a youth-oriented

culture to one of middle-aged and older adults. In the midst of this "age wave," the church is offered an unusual opportunity for ministry and growth. We are living in an *unprecedented* era of history where the needs, interests, and resources of those we define as "senior adults" will dominate our society, our families, and our churches.[1]

Not Done Yet

I don't remember her name, but I'll never forget meeting a medical missionary at a Christian writers' conference when I was 25. She was in her 70s and had spent a good deal of her life in India. Although she was rather frail physically, her attitude was vibrant and youthful. Her stories of the Lord's faithfulness in a hostile environment had a great influence on my spiritual growth. She was no longer on the mission field, but she was still serving the Lord by her example.

These great men and women of God, just by their examples, gave me a great gift: the knowledge that we always have a family in our fellow Christians and that God considers us useful as long as we live. As one person said, "If God were finished with me, He'd have already taken me to heaven." Whether we're active at 80 or bedridden at 60, we don't ever retire from the Lord's work. He wants to use us all, whatever our circumstances. God shows us in the Bible that He uses older adults in many ways. He often called upon older believers, including Moses, Abraham, Caleb, Anna, and Simeon.

When men and women, who have survived seven or eight decades of life, model Christlike behavior and serve as examples of Christian maturity, their lives can have an enormous impact on others. Who else can describe God's faithfulness with as many years of experience behind them? Who else can encourage the younger generation so unconditionally? With the responsibilities of raising children completed and the demands of a career behind them, older Christians are an invaluable bank of resources to our churches.

One San Diego church sponsors three different levels of senior ministries: "Go-Go, Slow-Go, and No-Go." Each of these senior ministries has consciously rejected the "rocking chair" philosophy that says, "I've worked hard all my life, let the younger generation take over." Even those who can't go anywhere minister as they can.

Redefining "Old"

Chronological age isn't nearly as important as how old a persons *feels, acts,* or *thinks.* Most healthy persons usually feel about 15 years younger than they are. Often when senior adults think about the word "old," they have someone else in mind. The former baseball pitcher Satchel Paige is famous for saying, "How old would you be if you didn't know how old you was?"

We see this spirit in the 90-year-old woman who was reviewing her finances with an accountant. When asked about a large sum of money in one account, she replied, "I'm saving that for my old age!"

Many persons define themselves as old when they begin to act old. Their steps slow down. They have trouble getting in and out of chairs. They groan in the process because their "bones" creak. They feel old, so they begin to act old.

But it is difficult to put a strict definition on "old." One can join the American Association of Retired Persons (AARP) when one turns 50. Restaurants regularly feature menus for "seniors"—those customers 55 and older. Social Security benefits are available at age 65, an arbitrary standard.

One person used this definition: "One good test of getting old is when you find yourself regularly showing off pictures of your grandchildren. Or try [this] test . . . While leaning over to tie your shoes, does your mind ask your body, 'Is there anything else I should be doing while I'm down here?'"[2]

Perhaps "old" has less to do with a numerical age or a designated group name than with people's attitudes—how they see themselves and what "old" means to them.

Using the Resources You Have

Ruth Barry, a member of a Holiness church in San Diego, developed a heart condition a few years ago, but the 84-year-old remains as active as possible and is a great believer in prayer.

She has learned to use even her immobile moments to serve God and others. "There's no need for you to sit down and look out the window when you grow old. This morning I was getting some tests at the hospital. Everywhere I go, I drop a little testimony to the nurses and technicians that I'm a Christian.

"Today I did a test—the doctor wanted to see how I was doing with this heart restriction. I had to lie with this picture-taking thing for 30 minutes. It took a picture every 20 seconds. I started praying for different people and different circumstances. And that 30 minutes just took a little while. Then I went on to another process and went back on the table for 25 minutes, and I found myself feeling that was a good time to finish praying."

She says seniors can also serve others by making calls and writing letters: "I'm trying to improve on this, but I feel if people are caring, they will find people who need a lift with a call or card or act of kindness, even if they can't get to them. There's a tremendous need for that."

She also participates in an all-ages, small care group at church. She thinks such groups are a great idea for seniors.

"Start with small care groups," she advises. "Don't be

timid, even if most are younger than you. There are Bible studies just for older women, but I like to be with the younger people. Otherwise, I never get to know them. That's a problem with some churches; they segregate people."

Keeping Interest Alive

"Scoots" Ayer, 78, has been active in church work since she was a teenager, and despite arthritis, hasn't slowed down much since. She and her husband, Harold, decided to give the Lord the first year of their retirement. When they were both 65, they went to Japan to teach English at Japan Christian Junior College in Chiba-ken. Now widowed, she's been missionary president for the church for 13 years and helps raise support and encourage missionaries.

"Sometimes I think it would be nice to slow down, but I'm too interested. There are too many interesting things to do," she says. "I have arthritis in my knees, and I walk like an old lady." She laughs, then continues, "It bothers me a lot, but I just don't want to quit.

"Entertaining and being a hostess at my home has been a hobby also. We've been fortunate in that we have had many missionaries stay at our home for days or weeks. That's been rewarding."

Ayer also makes calligraphy card-stock plaques that read "Prayer Changes Things." She decorates them with pressed flowers and sends them to missionaries to use as gifts.

A Rich Diversity

Evangelist Janine Tartaglia, who served as a minister to senior adults in Pasadena, California, for eight years, is writing a book about her experience with senior ministries. The program, with a philosophy of ministering both to and through seniors, grew from 55 to hundreds during that time.

The seniors chose the name "Forerunners" for their group, an appropriate name because the basic purpose of the ministry was to declare God's power to the next generation. Their logo included the message "Senior Adults inspired to set a Christlike example in prayer, praise, and service." Seniors were encouraged to participate in four important functions of the church: worship, nurturing, fellowship, and outreach.

On worship, Tartaglia writes: "It is no surprise that senior adults who maintain a close relationship with God are better able to cope with the trials of aging. Those who regularly humble themselves before God seem to have a more positive outlook about themselves and others. Essentially, the fruit of worship is a changed life, one that continually submits to God's pruning toward perfection . . . Whether at a banquet, on a trip, making crafts, or visiting the sick, seniors should be encouraged to pray and testify about what God is doing in their lives today."

She says of nurturing: "Senior adults who have influenced me the most are those who admit they are still learning. They also take the time to pass on what they've learned to others. A senior adult ministry should provide many opportunities to grow in Christ and share His light and love with others."

On fellowship: "As mentioned earlier, all of our gatherings are accented by prayer, song, and testimony. They also enable seniors of different ages, income levels, and backgrounds to become better acquainted."

Outreach is essential, according to Tartaglia: "Since Jesus put no age limit on the Great Commission, senior adults are not excused to 'mark time' before He returns. Instead, they are to join younger believers in 'going out and making disciples' . . . Since there are about 70 retirement homes in the greater Pasadena area, our Forerunner ministry is aware of a vast harvest of elderly people who are running out of time to enter God's kingdom."[3]

Tartaglia describes some of the various groups and ministries started to achieve the goals above.

"We had a ministry called 'Love Line' where people would call to check on the shut-ins. Many seniors ended up doing this calling themselves. And soon, shut-ins were calling other shut-ins. Eventually, shut-ins, rather than waiting for someone else to minister to them, began ministering to others. One lady's life really turned around, and she became head of the ministry. Other seniors, in teams of two, would go out and visit other seniors. This was the 'Sunshine Company.'"

Seniors could join other small groups, such as the Early Christians, who met weekly for prayer at 6 A.M., or the Prayer Warriors, a group of shut-ins who received a weekly list of prayer requests from members of the church family. There were also support, social, exercise, and devotion groups.

"Another ministry we had was the Forerunner Family Ties. The seniors would go into younger Sunday School classes and have families fill out a profile card. We had 200 seniors cover young families with prayer. This was an effective way to get to know the next generation.

"Our seniors do the adopting," she explains. "Rather than waiting to be adopted as a grandparent, they adopt a teen or a younger person in the church. They pass love and encouragement on to others. They see themselves as passing on what they have learned."

Another popular activity Tartaglia recalls was a regular monthly banquet that drew up to 450 people. After the dinner, a Christian singer would perform and give an altar call.

"These events weren't just for us but were designed to glorify God," she says. "We emphasized outreach and encouraged people to bring friends. Some people were saved through our banquets.

"We as a church can help with the perception of aging. So often seniors themselves don't have an image of productivity. They are encouraged to let the younger ones take over. There is a time for that, to let go of the reins; but seniors still need to be involved.

"We in the church also need to take a good look at 'what is productivity?' Is it always action, or is it effectively modeling Christlike behavior? One of the most effective ways seniors can minister to the congregation is by example of Christian maturity—a genuine faith, contentment in any circumstance, a gentle, caring spirit, a positive, encouraging outlook," she continues.

"Sometimes we have a distorted view of a person's worth if our identities are measured in productivity. I'm just as concerned with those seniors who are extremely active in the body but do not exemplify Christ's spirit—we can see this when things don't go the way they wish, or they aren't in control. How we express ourselves—our attitude—is so important in modeling Christian maturity and Christlike behavior.

"I think of Harold Platt, a missionary to India for 40 years. He came home and cared for his wife who had Alzheimer's. Then he got leukemia. He remained, through his last days, a light, positive, and praising Christian. The young people in our church adored him."

She describes a woman she calls Grandma Estelle Crutcher, now 94, her pastor's mother-in-law. "She discipled me to a true, sanctified walk with Christ when she was in her 80s, and she continues to hold me accountable."

As Janine Tartaglia's experiences and the testimony of

many Christian seniors show, there are numerous ways we can continue to serve God and our families, no matter what our health or circumstances. Whether we are 25 or 75, whether we are a prayer warrior, an active volunteer, or an avid encourager, we never outgrow our usefulness in God's eyes. Seniors can have a tremendous impact on others when they glorify God and serve as witnesses of His love.

NOTES

1. Win and Charles Arn, "Riding the Wave of Silver and Gray," *Leadership* (Fall 1990): 112.

2. Win Arn, *Live Long and Love It!* (Wheaton, Ill.: Tyndale House Publishers, 1991), 4-5.

3. Janine Tartaglia, "The Age Wave: Senior Adult Ministries in the '90s," pamphlet written for First Church of the Nazarene, Pasadena, Calif.

THE QUESTION

"Father, has my life made a difference?"

THE ISSUES

- I feel like a "nobody." Am I really worthless?
- Did all my work through the years amount to nothing?
- If we are all equal in God's sight, why are some people considered to be more important than others?

BACKGROUND SCRIPTURE:

1 Cor. 3:6; Heb. 10:36; 11

13

Will I Only Be Remembered if My Name's in the News?

by Doug Williams

WE KNOW WHO they are.
They are the ones who are always recognized in magazines for doing extraordinary things. They are the power brokers with the high profile jobs. The movers and shakers. They know that they're touching lives because they can see themselves in the news. They get strokes every day for the things they accomplish, while the rest of us struggle from paycheck to paycheck, hoping our car will make it home one more time. With all the struggles we have in our lives, we begin to ask ourselves if it really matters. Will anyone really notice, or care, if I just stop?

Doug Williams is a certified counselor working at Christian Counseling Services in Nashville. He and his wife, Amy, have one son.

A Case Study

Let me tell you about Mary.* She is an attractive, middle-aged woman who is very successful in running her own business. Divorced from her husband, she is having some struggles in raising her children. Crises seem to come in bunches for Mary. Her son has some attention difficulty and has had to work harder in school just to keep up. Her daughter is pregnant and is looking to place the child for adoption. The man she had been dating is seeing someone else, and the hope that she had for a life with him is quickly fading. She is confused. She is active in her church, but life continues to treat her unfairly.

This has been the pattern for her, dating back to her abusive childhood. Any of these issues, by themselves, could be depressing. Life experiences have a tendency to spill over into other areas of life. Put them all together, add in low self-esteem, and they can be devastating.

She asks if her life matters. Will it really matter, in the big picture, if she were not around? Who will miss her if she is gone? What kind of a legacy is she giving her children? She knows, intellectually, that she is a child of God and that she is important to Him. But is she really important to anyone else? She rarely feels that way. She asks, "How much of a Kingdom effect am I having on this world? Or am I just going through the motions, waiting for this life to end so I can go on to the next?"

Another Case Study

Now let me tell you about Bob.* He is a plumber who defied the odds and became a Christian at age 38. His wife and children prayed that God would change his life, and God did.

Bob is not the typical Christian, and I'm thankful for that. He is 62 years old, and his hobby is racing his vintage motorcycle, a 350 Honda. His goals in racing are simple—

to stay upright and finish the race. He is pretty successful at attaining those goals. I doubt that Bob has ever met a stranger. If he has, the person stayed a stranger only by choice. He is comfortable with nearly anyone he meets and is genuine in his love and concern for others.

Because he loves people, he is willing to help those that ask for his assistance with their plumbing needs. Leaky faucets, stopped-up drains, anything to help. He doesn't limit it to plumbing needs. Manual labor and Bob are closely related.

Bob has problems too. Divorces have occurred in his family. His parents have died, as have a younger brother and a daughter-in-law. But he has a faith in God that has sustained him through these and other problems.

When Bob dies—may it not be soon!—we will see a wide range of people at his funeral. We are just as likely to see missionaries and pastors there as to see his riding buddies. The clothing styles of the people will be the only obvious difference. Ministers and motorcycle riders rarely dress anything alike.

But both groups will say, "Bob was a great guy who loved God. He loved people with the love of the Lord." Bob's daily walk, regardless of the struggles, is evidence that he is not living under his own power or authority. He had tried that before, and it didn't work. Bob isn't concerned about his effect on the Kingdom. He is living as God wants him to live and letting God do the rest.

When Do I Start Feeling This Way, and Why?

Let's consider what may be going on with someone who is uncertain that his or her life has meaning. When do we feel that way? Why? What does it take to get beyond that feeling?

Most people will have a feeling of insignificance at some point in their lives. If they don't, they are probably not being honest. Because we are human, we as Christians will sometimes have questions regarding our effectiveness for the Kingdom. These times usually come after some event that doesn't go as we had hoped. We may get overly invested in someone's life. When things don't go well, we take too much responsibility for the results.

Let's go back to Mary. When things go wrong for her, the first question she asks is, "What's wrong with *me* that this event turned out this way?" The circumstances don't matter to her. She feels something must be wrong with her for this to have happened. She can come up with many reasons why she is responsible for things that aren't totally her fault. She might have made some contributions to the event, but she takes *all* the blame for any crisis that happens. This leads her deeper into her sense of low self-esteem, and the question of her importance to the Kingdom returns.

When we take more than our share of responsibility over the events that affect our lives, we get overwhelmed. When that happens, we lose the balance between our responsibility and God's responsibility. Our job is to follow. He is in charge of the results of our following His will. We lose track of this when we walk only by sight and always expect that we will see the results of our work for the Kingdom. Charles Swindoll asks: "But since when do people of faith conduct their lives on the basis of sight?"[1]

Balance—What Is It, and Where Do I Order It?

In Matt. 5:13-16, Jesus says:

You are the salt of the earth. But if the salt loses its saltiness, how can it be made salty again? It is no longer good for anything, except to be thrown out and trampled by men. You are the light of the world. A city on a hill cannot be hidden. Neither do people light a lamp and put it under a bowl. Instead they put it on its stand, and it gives light to everyone in the house. In the same way, let your light shine before men, that they may see your good deeds and praise your Father in heaven.

By calling us salt and light, Jesus has expectations for us to have a positive effect on this world for the Kingdom. His expectations are that we light the house we are in, not necessarily the whole neighborhood. God will be sure to let us know how big our area is to light. He won't leave us groping around in the dark and wondering what our responsibility is. Whatever our house turns out to be, He expects us to be a light in it so people will see the Father.

Our lives are supposed to make a difference to the people around us. But if we're concerned about whether or not our lives have made a difference, we're concerned about the wrong thing. Let me explain.

One of the definitions that my *American Heritage Dictionary* gives for "concern" is: "To cause anxiety or uneasiness in; to trouble."[2] If we are concerned about how our lives are affecting others, we may be anxious about things not in our control. We may begin thinking that we are responsible for the results of our interactions, but we aren't. God is. We do have the responsibility to be salt and light, but we do not determine how others are affected by it. If we are following God's will for our lives, the effect our lives have on others will be determined by God. Remember what Paul said in 1 Cor. 3:6, "I planted the seed, Apollos watered it, but God made it grow."

That's where the balance is: Being responsible to God for our obedience, but letting God do with our obedience what He wants.

Resting in the Balance

We have no guarantee that we will ever see the "fruit of [our] labour" (Phil. 1:22, KJV). Some will, some won't. If we are resting in the promises of God, we can trust Him to do what He says He will do. God is faithful. We need to remember Heb. 11, the great faith chapter. The writer of that book says that "all these people were living by faith when they died. They did not receive the things promised; they only saw them . . . from a distance" (v. 13). He was talking about Abraham, Sarah, Isaac, Jacob, Joseph, and Moses. They were all given the same promise that God would make a great nation of them, and that He would provide salvation for the world from their line. And He did.

When—not if—we feel discouraged, we can rest on the promise of Heb. 10:36, which reads, "You need to persevere so that when you have done the will of God, you will receive what he has promised."

Did He promise that faithful Christians would be newsmakers? No, He has promised rest for our souls. Even if our names are never in the headlines, we can do His will every day.

NOTES

*Name has been changed.
1. Charles Swindoll, *Living Above the Level of Mediocrity* (Dallas: Word Publishing, 1987), 98.
2. *The American Heritage Dictionary*, 2nd ed., s.v. "concern."

OTHER DIALOG SERIES BOOKS

A Christian Attitude Toward Attitudes

Christian Personality Under Construction

Christians at Work in a Hurting World

Christians in a Crooked World

Clean Living in a Dirty World

Growing Season: Maturing of a Christian

How to Improve Your Prayer Life

How to Live the Holy Life

I Believe: Now Tell Me Why

Less Stress, Please

Misguiding Lights? The Gospel According to . . .

No Easy Answers: Christians Debate Today's Issues

Questions You Shouldn't Ask About Christianity

Questions You Shouldn't Ask About the Church

Raising Kids

Spiritual Zest: Finding It and Keeping It

The Me I See: A Christian Approach to Self-Esteem

Turning Points—That Can Make Us or Break Us

What Jesus Said About . . .

When Life Gets Rough

For a description of all available Dialog Series books, including some that may not be listed here, ask for a free brochure from your favorite Christian bookstore, your denominational distributor, or Beacon Hill Press of Kansas City.